THE SERENITY
Mindset

THE SERENITY
Mindset

A Personal Guide for Prioritizing
People and Things That Matter

Joyce,
May your
life be filled with much
serenity!

Nancy M. Forbes

With
blessings,
Nancy

Alpharetta, GA

ISBN: 978-1-61005-521-5

Library of Congress Control Number: 2016919565

10 9 8 7 6 5 4 3 2   0 1 0 9 1 7

Printed in the United States of America

♾This paper meets the requirements of ANSI/NISO Z39.48-1992 (Permanence of Paper)

In Loving Memory of:

Tracy, the epitome of what "to have a good friend, you must be a good friend" really means. I hope you knew how important you were to me, and that I showed you my love. Thank you for all of the wonderful memories and lessons. Your memory will always be alive in me!

AND

Zorro, my canine best friend and loyal companion. It just was not the same without my writing buddy beside me as I finished writing. I hope you found a wonderful soft and sunny spot at Rainbow Bridge where the "dogs" are not bothering you; we all know you never regarded yourself as one of them.

Dedicated to:

Lew, the love of my life. Thank you for your patience, your willingness and desire to work on "us," and for always making me your number one in life. I love you with all my heart, and hope you know that you are my number one as well.

AND

All of the people who have been a part of my life at some point in time, but especially those of you who have left footprints in my heart. My life is so much richer because of you.

Peace is a daily, a weekly, a monthly process, gradually changing opinions, slowly eroding old barriers, quietly building new structures. And however undramatic the pursuit of peace, that pursuit must go on.

—John F. Kennedy

Contents

Acknowledgments

TOOLS AND RESOURCES

About the Author

Introduction

As humans, every one of us will confront challenges in our lives; there is no set path anyone can take to avoid obstacles. But when faced with difficult experiences, each of us must make the choice to either turn away from them, or embrace and address them. It is from challenges that we learn and grow.

The Serenity Mindset is the story of my personal metamorphosis of self-healing after losing a dear friend, my career/identity, and my husband in a nine-month period of time. Having always been a relatively strong person when it came to handling difficult situations, I found myself anything but, and instead was overwhelmed with both loss and rejection.

Through my trifecta of losses, I learned some life-changing lessons about serenity and relationships that I continue to practice each day. In *The Serenity Mindset*, I share the simple techniques I used myself for stilling my mind and recognizing what I can and cannot change, and allocating my time and effort on the things and the people that have a positive effect on my overall well-being.

There are things and people we cannot change, so why waste energy there? I love the tree analogy that Tyler Perry uses as he thinks of people in different situations in his life, which he refers to as his tree test:

What Kind of Person Are You?
By Tyler Perry

LEAF PEOPLE

Some people come into your life and they are like leaves on a tree. They are only there for a season. You can't depend on them or count on them because they are weak and only there to give you shade. Like leaves, they are there to take what they need and as soon as it gets cold or a wind blows in your life they are gone. You can't be angry at them, it's just who they are.

BRANCH PEOPLE

There are some people who come into your life and they are like branches on a tree. They are stronger than leaves, but you have to be careful with them. They will stick around through most seasons, but if you go through a storm or two in your life it's possible that you could lose them. Most times they break away when it's tough. Although they are stronger than leaves, you have to test them out before you run out there and put all your weight on them. In most cases they can't handle too much weight. But again, you can't be mad with them, it's just who they are.

ROOT PEOPLE

If you can find some people in your life who are like the roots of a tree then you have found something special. Like the roots of a tree, they are hard to find because they are not trying to be seen. Their only job is to hold you up and help you live a strong and healthy life. If you thrive, they are happy. They stay low key and don't let the world know that they are there. And if you go through an awful storm they will hold you up. Their job is to hold you up, come what may, and to nourish you, feed you, and water you.

Just as a tree has many limbs and many leaves, there are few roots. Look at your own life. How many leaves, branches, and roots do you have? What are you in other people's lives?

THANK GOD FOR YOUR ROOTS! You may want to call them today or share this message with them and attach your own note saying, "Thanks for being my root."[1]

With time as one of our most precious commodities, my hope is that after reading this book, not only will you have a better appreciation of how healthy having genuine relationships is for you, but also more insight into how you can focus your time and efforts on the things and people that make your life meaningful, while mitigating the chance for regrets at the same time.

PART ONE

A Trifecta of Losses

1
Losing My Friend

It was January 2013. I was in my midfifties and miserable. I did not like the person I had become. My misery started to carry over into how I acted and thus was perceived by other people in my life. I do not know why I did not seek help—perhaps because that would require too much effort, or maybe I did not even realize how bad off I really was.

Midmonth, I would be getting together with nine college friends for our biannual four-day "YaYa reunion." Between our history together and the depth of reunion conversations among this nonjudgmental, safe, and caring group of friends, we knew just about everything about each other, including if something was wrong. It was clear to them how unhappy I was. They were determined to see that I got professional counseling as soon as possible.

I started to see a counselor two weeks after the reunion. Thank goodness I had her to turn to because little did I know that, as miserable as I was then, things were about to get much worse.

Teresa's Tragic Passing

You never know when you will lose a very dear friend. We go through life, and for whatever reason, never really think that we will die until we reach a ripe old age. Yes, there are those that die in freak accidents, or through rare illnesses, but we tend to justify those as exceptions in our minds.

That is, until I tragically lost my friend Teresa. Ironically I had already said goodbye to her, as she was moving overseas for a few years, but never did I suspect it would be our final goodbye. Then one morning, less than two months after our see-you-soon goodbye, my healthy, fifty-year-old friend did not wake up. While this may be the peaceful way we all hope to pass, it was much too early, and much too painful, for she left behind a delightful three-year-old daughter.

I knew something was wrong when my husband came home from work midmorning, as he would never have done that unless he had forgotten something important. I was already sitting down, or else he probably would have insisted I do so. He said, "I have some bad news . . . Teresa died." Thinking he could not possibly be talking about my friend Teresa, I asked, "Teresa who?" His face and eyes said it all as he, too, was very fond of her. In a state of shock himself, he thought he had misheard what Teresa's husband said to him on the phone when he got the call because her husband could not reach me.

I was in a state of shock and disbelief, as were many others. Some of Teresa's closest friends, myself included, rallied to the best of our abilities under the circumstances to help the family in any way possible to get through the memorial services. Hundreds of people came to pay their respects and to celebrate Teresa's life. She had done so much for so many people throughout the world.

Teresa had a way of showing a special love for each individual and making that person feel more special than anyone ever made them feel, so of course that made for a unique bond between that person and her. In fact, the theme of her eulogy was about how everyone looked at her as "my Teresa."

I was reminded during this difficult time that "the only thing stronger than loss is love." Because "our Teresa" had touched us all with her love, we would ultimately find strength through all of the many wonderful memories, though that would take some time.

The Defining Moment

I was really struggling with this loss. Teresa and I had been like sisters. We first met as colleagues at a large corporation where we readily hit it off, both being instigators who worked really hard but also liked to have fun, even if we were in a very conservative business environment. We became kindred spirits who shared the love of snowmen, pumpkins, autumn, angels, hugs, flowers, the golden rule, travel, food and wine, arts and crafts, and the list goes on. We talked openly about every topic imaginable, and always felt energized in the end regardless of how delicate the topic might have been. We shared many of each other's life events, and more lunches together than most people will ever hope to have in a lifetime.

This was the first time I had ever lost a friend who was a contemporary. Knowing that I would never talk to her or see her again left me feeling at a loss. I was wishing we could have one more conversation, and I started to think about what I would say to her if that wish was ever granted.

I would tell her what a wonderful friend she was. In fact, I would tell her she was what I now recognize as a "best friend." I would tell her how much I enjoyed sharing all the times we laughed and cried together, all the fun things we tried, and all the not-so-fun things that we survived. I would tell her how much I appreciated how we were able to share anything—values, feelings, confessions—no matter how scary the topic was to bring up, or how vulnerable it might have made us feel. I would thank her for her shared part in openly and honestly helping each other achieve a deeper understanding of self. I would tell her how much I will miss the heartfelt, reflective, and energized feeling after being open and vulnerable with her, someone who I completely trusted.

I was both sad and surprised that I did not have this defining moment until her death. When my father passed away suddenly, I learned the importance of leaving nothing unsaid to my mother and the rest of my family, but sadly I never thought to carry this lesson over to the other relationships in my life. I guess the big difference is that I always recognized how important my family was to me; until Teresa's death, I never really reflected on how the relationships in my life varied from one another.

Was this realization of not proactively reflecting on relationships unique to me? I certainly wanted to learn from this lesson so I could be sure to treat those most special to me accordingly; I did not want to repeat this feeling of being too late with things unsaid or undone. I was convinced others could benefit from this revelation as well, so I made a note to myself to explore my relationships in greater detail once I got to a point where my head was clearer. The least I could do at this time was to try to turn this difficult lesson learned into something beneficial.

Keeping Her Memory Alive

It tore at my heart knowing that Teresa's little girl, Myra, would grow up without really knowing her wonderful mother who had already taught her so much, and guided and encouraged her to be a very unique three-year-old.

While you are limited with the relationship you can have with a three-year-old, Myra was very comfortable with me, having joined her mother and me for many lunches and visits. In fact, before their move, I took Myra on a special, full-day Christmastime outing so that Teresa could focus on packing. We formed a special bond that day.

I very much wanted to stay a part of Myra's life going forward, and share with her some of the things that her mom and I enjoyed together. Already showing an interest in coloring and music, I thought it would be nice to somehow find a way to regularly expose Myra to arts and entertainment. I would have to try to work out some way to make that happen.

2
Losing My Career

After Teresa's passing, I had found it very difficult to focus on things at work. Her death only made me realize how unimportant this work really was. I was not doing anything that made the world a better place, or helped to save lives. It was all like a game.

I had been especially unhappy at work the last three years. In fact, at the first session with my counselor, she gave me the homework assignment to write out why I was staying in a job that made me so miserable. I thought about it and jotted down some notes to discuss with her, but we never had that talk because when we regrouped a few weeks later, being miserable at work was the least of my concerns. I was then deeply grieving the loss of my very dear friend, Teresa.

The Way It Was

I began my career with the company in 1980 in Tucson, Arizona. I turned down the programmer position they offered me because I just could not envision myself tied to a computer day in and day out, instead accepting a position in cost accounting. It is ironic to think about that now given how much we have all become so tied to and dependent on computers.

I learned a great deal, met many fascinating people, and truly enjoyed my first twenty years at this corporation. During all of that time, I worked in a traditional office environment, both while I was in Arizona and after I transferred to Georgia.

Colleagues worked and played hard together. We were genuinely interested in working as a team, through which we formed bonds that benefitted both the individual and the company. Because of this, the business was a stellar example of the formula for success: *Satisfied/Happy Employees Lead to Satisfied/Happy Customers and Stockholders, Which Lead to Company Success.*

Team building used to be a high priority. We had some wonderful team-building outings. Whether we were at a nearby park doing facilitated team exercises, having an annual kickoff picnic, or going on a river-rafting trip, our bonds grew both inside and outside of work. Some of these connections led to friendships that are still in existence many years later.

While many of us are no longer with the company, we still try to all get together at least once a year for an annual holiday gathering. At that get-together, we go around the circle taking turns to update the group on each of our highs and lows throughout the year. It is always a fun evening filled with all kinds of emotions.

I recall the first holiday gathering after Teresa's death. We had a great turnout. It was a very moving evening. She had always been a bubbly and fun person at this event. It was obvious she was missing in more ways than one. We remembered her when we said grace, and we also had a good sob over the lesson she had taught us about how important it is to make time for friendships. One of the girls who had not regularly attended in the past was so touched by this lesson in friendship that she vowed to never miss the annual event again.

The Internet Effect on the Work Environment

Early in the twenty-first century, the Internet greatly enhanced the ability to work from almost anywhere. While this wonderful technology increased the opportunities for jobs you could now qualify for, it also significantly changed the work environment. Face-to-face conversations began to be replaced with conference calls. Over time, with work and people geographically dispersed, much of one's workday was spent on the phone. I got to where I despised talking to anyone on the phone after work, even with friends and family, because that is what I had done all day!

With technology enabling one to work from almost anywhere, it also opened up the ability to work from home. This would be the answer to my dream of being there when my sons came home from school during those challenging teenage years. What a blessing! This gave me the flexibility during the day to throw in a load of wash, fold clothes, do dinner prep—all while I was on conference calls. While this may sound really great, it was also very isolating.

This type of nontraditional office brought about a whole new meaning to "workday." Between peers located all around the world, and the numerous jobs that had been sent overseas to developing economies, we were having conference calls with colleagues across worldwide time zones. It was not unusual to have very-early-morning as well as very-late-night calls. It had become obvious that the price for this increased flexibility was a sort of enslavement with longer hours, constantly spent on the phone, and the expectation of 24/7 availability.

Unfortunately, the Internet-enabled ability to work remotely also had a huge adverse impact on team dynamics, teamwork, and communication. Unlike in the traditional work environment where in-person bonds potentially led to friendships, in a virtual workplace that seldom happened. There were rarely even chitchat opportunities to try to get to know each other because workers quickly got off one conference call, and started on the next almost immediately. And far be it from anyone to build time into the day for idle conversation when being scheduled with back-to-back calls had become the de facto measure of busyness and thus "importance."

Time was not the only factor that kept people from getting to know each other. Because of travel expense restrictions that were imposed each year, it was not unusual that you never met project or team colleagues face-to-face. As a result, many of my business acquaintances over these years were nothing more than a voice to me.

Believe it or not, there was even a time when more than two years passed before I actually met my immediate manager who was responsible for coaching and appraising me. It was irrational to think this kind of arrangement would work satisfactorily for either the manager or the employee. For a company that publicly heralded their employees to be its greatest assets, we had been reduced to serial numbers and voices on the phone.

The Cultural Effect of Downsizing and Acquisitions

Downsizing had been going on in this particular company since early in the twenty-first century. "Resource actions" — what became code for "layoffs" — became part of the "corporate culture" there, as the company exercised this method of "efficiency" multiple times each year. At the onset, downsizings would make the news headlines because of the thousands of workers that were affected. Then companies became savvier and started to resort to more piecemeal downsizing so that the total magnitude of jobs being sent out of the country was more difficult for those on the outside to calculate.

At the same time that the existing workforce was being decreased, there were many acquisitions taking place that brought workers onboard from very different corporate cultures. Most of the time there was not a formal program to integrate the employees from different heritages into that of the existing culture. What was once an enviably strong culture had now eroded to a very blended, almost nonculture.

The human impact of layoffs had a huge effect on the work environment. Employees naturally turned inward to focus on self-protection. While there was still talk about the importance of teamwork, recognition went to individuals, cultivating a very self-centered, competitive culture. Team building was no longer considered important, and genuine friendships between colleagues outside of work became more and more rare.

It had become a very toxic, cutthroat environment. I found myself forced to compete against people who were so self-focused that they thought nothing of doing things that, in my opinion, put personal values in question. It was nothing for managers to compliment you on the creativity of an idea and then "borrow" it to pitch up the executive line, without any recognition to the original source.

As a result of a combination of all these factors, after thirty years of being a high achiever and often times far exceeding expectations, my performance reviews during my last three years were not as stellar. I dreaded being there. I did not fit in, nor did I want to.

A Definite Target

While I had managed to dodge many of the down-sizing bullets across the years, I knew this time that I was a definite target given my age, years with the company, and salary. After all these years you think you would be "prepared" for when your time to get "hit" comes, but there really is no way to brace yourself to be told that your services are no longer needed.

Along came the day that I received an e-mail invitation for a fifteen-minute conference call with my manager. I knew that it was related to the resource action underway. Waiting out the days before the scheduled call seemed endless, so when the day of my call finally arrived, it was almost a relief.

I called in to the designated conference call number, and there were already two people on the call—my manager and a representative from the legal department.

It was now just four months after Teresa's passing, and here I was being told that because of a restructuring in the business, my job was being eliminated and therefore the company no longer needed my services. My manager added that fortunately I was "retirement eligible," so I would be getting a call from the employee services group for help in handling the transition to retirement.

After years of dodging the bullet, I was now one of the many hundreds of thousands impacted by yet another of the numerous cost-efficient "resource actions."

What Next?

You never realize how much of your identity is associated with your work until you no longer have that role. Having been so miserable, on one hand it felt like I had been released from prison. But on the other hand, there was a hurtful feeling of rejection after giving so much of myself for thirty-three years. It was like a divorce, and another loss in my life—this time my career instead of my friend Teresa.

You may recall that at my first visit to the counselor, she had asked me to write out why I was staying in a job that made me feel so miserable. When I went to see her the week after the resource action, it was almost humorous when she told me that the good news was we were rid of the impetus of my original unhappiness ... my job!

Several former colleagues who were friends that had gone through past resource actions willingly offered advice and comfort. Ironically, they were all about the same age with the same or more years of service. How so many corporations were getting away with this obvious age discrimination still dumbfounds me! But I did not want to exert the energy to fight that battle. With so much of it going on, there had to be some loophole that was protecting corporations that targeted their layoffs by age as they shipped hundreds of thousands of jobs overseas.

It was a very weird feeling when I was at a doctor's appointment after being laid off. I was filling out the required paperwork and got to the place where it asked for occupation. That is when the reality of my lost identity really hit me. While it really did not necessarily matter how I filled in the space, I left it blank, and that emptiness is exactly how I felt.

While over the years I had done many self-assessments to discover my passion, nothing ever really jumped out at me because of my many diverse interests. I felt as though I just needed some time to myself at this point, to process everything.

It is funny how we always think we are in control of our destiny, and then something happens to reassure us we are not. Almost immediately after my last day at work, I received a call from my brother saying that my younger sister had suffered a very bad fall down a flight of stairs and was in the hospital. She was going to need help when she returned home. That became the answer to what was most immediately in store for me next.

I headed to my hometown in Massachusetts to stay with her about ten days. I was so grateful to be in a position where I could help. If I had still been working, it would not have been so easy to do. Being disciplined with her physical therapy, my sister became stronger each day, and by the time I left, I knew she would be fine.

When I returned home, I felt good about having helped my sister in her time of need, but the reality of not having my normal work routine set in quickly. Still grieving the losses of both Teresa and my career during a four-month period, I was feeling somewhat bitter and insecure. My mind was not helping matters, as it conjured up all kinds of worst-case scenarios of what would lie ahead for me.

On a walk one morning it struck me. I had always said that when I retired, one of the first things I was going to do was to go through each room in the house and clean. So now that I was officially "retired," I figured I might as well get started.

I have always been a big list person. I absolutely LOVE being able to cross through completed items on the list with a thick marker! So the first thing that I did was to make a list of all that needed to be done in each room for cleaning and decluttering, as well as all the other projects I had been wanting to do for a long time but never had the time to do.

Cleaning is therapeutic in its own sort of way, allowing you time to think about things. It was the perfect project to allow me time to ponder what I was going to do next with my life, which I referred to as "Act 2." The timing would be just right for me to be able to finish the cleaning before heading off to Bermuda with my husband, Lew, and our two sons to celebrate our twenty-fifth wedding anniversary.

3
Losing My Husband

We had a wonderful time in Bermuda. It was fun to reexplore and see what had and had not changed since our time there twenty-five years ago on our honeymoon. Enjoying the time with our sons, we snorkeled, rode mopeds, kayaked, toured, enjoyed many of the island's infamous rum-based swizzle sticks, and just relaxed.

When we returned home from Bermuda, my life took a spin I had never seen coming. On our actual anniversary a couple of weeks later, I asked my husband if he would marry me again, and he replied that he did not know. He went on to say that he was not happy and had not been for a while. He said that he needed time to think because this was not how he wanted to spend the rest of his life.

I was dumbfounded. While I knew that things could be better between us, I had no idea he was so miserable.

Twenty-Five Years Earlier

My husband and I started out as casual friends long before our relationship became romantic. We met at work when he approached me in my role in the accounting department to ask me how much I was estimating for the month's bad-debts write-off. Since he was responsible for projecting the cash flow, he said that he wanted to take my amount into consideration in his estimate.

Each month following, we would have a personal bet between us as to who would come closest to estimating the actual amount of bad debts. The loser of the bet would have to pay for lunch! We enjoyed each other's company, and looked forward to the monthly lunch regardless of who paid for it. Over time, the friendship developed into a romantic relationship as well, and we ended up getting married and raising two wonderful sons together.

Unlike many couples, we did not have a few years with just the two of us early in our marriage. We had our first son within the first year, and the other thirteen months later. We always jokingly said that we had a late start, so we needed to be on the fast track! Between the challenges of a new marriage, a new home, two babies, the illness and death of my mother in between the boys' births, and two demanding careers, it was stressful, to say the least.

Fortunately, we were pretty much equal partners with work around the house and in life in general, so we made it work. Not only were we extremely involved in the boys' hectic schedules of activities, but we also managed to continue to do many of the things we enjoyed as well. Looking back, perhaps we were too busy for everyone else and not each other. Regardless, people we knew looked at us as a rock-solid couple who would never have marital problems.

Leaving Me

The discussion we had on our actual twenty-fifth wedding anniversary caught me completely off guard. Unlike me, my husband was the type that held things inside until it became unbearable. Hearing him say that he was not happy and had not been for a while immediately made me think there had to be another woman in his life because that is the typical story that follows those words.

He insisted there was not another person, but instead that he was tired of being treated with such little respect. He said that no one deserves such treatment, and he was right. The last three years of work in that toxic environment turned me into a different person. I hated the person that I had become, and it had carried over to how I communicated with the people in my life, especially my husband, who had patiently tolerated it until now.

He said that he needed to get away for a while to think things through. So he left on a road trip, not knowing where exactly he was going, or when he would be back. I tried to be understanding and not interruptive during this time of reflection. All along I thought for sure that he would come back and suggest we work things out, unless there was in fact another woman, in which case, who knew what he would say.

He returned after five days. When I asked him what he had decided, he said that he thought we should separate for a while. Needless to say I was devastated. I begged him not to leave, insisting I would be different. So he stayed until my next outburst when I lost my composure over some little thing. He left very late that night and would not say where he was going.

PART TWO

Looking Inward for Serenity

4
Acceptance and Trust

I cried until I could cry no longer, and then started to pray more than I ever have, asking for help and guidance, as I did not know which way to turn.

While I was brought up as a Catholic, I have since exposed myself to other religions. There is an anonymous quote that nicely summarizes my view of religion: "Buddha was not a Buddhist. Jesus was not a Christian. Muhammad was not a Muslim. They were teachers who taught love."

Throughout my life, I have always believed in a Spirit that I call God. It makes it easier for me to talk or pray to something with a name. And I continue to read, meditate, and participate in discussions to learn more about this God. To me, it does not matter what religious beliefs one has. What matters is that one believes and trusts, and I believe and trust in my God.

So it came as no surprise that I would increase my conversations with God during this difficult time and be in search of help to understand how I was feeling. I came across a poem called "Footprints in the Sand" by Mary Stevenson, which relates the story of one questioning

God being there for him when needed, evidenced by only one set of footprints in the sand instead of two. The doubt disappeared with the revelation that there is only one set of footprints when God is carrying you in time of need.

It resonated with me because I too was having some huge doubts, and felt my trust being tested. I knew, in fact, that I had reached the point of not being able to accept anything more being thrown at me, and was wondering where God was. So help the next person who said "God doesn't give you more than you can handle." While well intended, I really did not need to hear that at this point.

One can believe that things happen randomly, or that there is a divine plan for your life. I have always believed that everything happens for a reason. As difficult as this trifecta of losses was for me—my dear friend, my career, and my husband—I knew that it would teach me something in the long run. As said by mythologist Joseph Campbell, "Where you stumble, there you find your treasure." In what felt like the crossroads of trust or distrust, I chose trust.

EVERY THING HAPPENS FOR A REASON

5
Stilling the Mind

Being pretty much a basket case at this point, I was hoping that my session with my counselor would help me find the answer to what I was supposed to be learning from all of these painful happenings. Surmising that the voices in my head with all their worldly "advice" were making matters even worse, she told me about Jon Kabat-Zinn's mindfulness-based stress reduction (MBSR). Based on ancient healing practices, this technique brings together mindfulness meditation and yoga in an eight-week intensive training program.

My counselor felt confident that "mindfulness meditation" would help me to stay more aware of the present moment and keep the crazy thoughts of the past and future from running around in my head. Ironically, within one week's time, three other unrelated people suggested mindful meditation to me as well. I did not need to be hit over the head with a two-by-four to figure out that I better find a class and enroll. Obviously I was getting a clear message to take this class!

I drove to the first session not knowing what to expect or what I had gotten myself into, or why so many people had suggested it to me. I found it interesting, and very unlike anything else I have experienced. For a long time, I had wanted to learn meditation, but it never made my priority list because I was, ironically, "too busy." With a clean slate in front of me and the benefits sounding like they were just what I needed, I could not afford to turn away now!

The highlight of the teachings to me was learning how to block out the crazies we all have in our heads, often referred to as "the monkey mind." Next time these voices come into your head, think about how all their "advice" is based on the past and future, but never in the present. The important thing we learned was how not to let those voices take control.

Meditation did not come naturally to me by any means, but I was determined and became very dedicated to make it part of my daily practice. I started to see a noticeable difference on the days I did not make the time for stillness. It is just like anything else in life. We all have the same twenty-four hours in a day, seven days a week, and twelve months a year. We make time for those things that are important to us within those hours.

As I started to move past the state of shock and hurt from my losses, I was able to do a more focused self-reflection. I became more mindful of things around me, and started to notice and enjoy more of life's little things that I was now taking time to actually notice. I had always been one to focus in the future, and now I was seeing all that I was missing.

At this same time, I returned to my daily journaling, which I had abandoned some time ago. Each day I also listed five things I was grateful for that day. Sometimes these were little things, like the sound of the birds early in the morning, or worms after the rain . . . the things I now was aware of by being in the present. Other times, they were bigger things, such as how grateful I was for those friends that were there to support me during this terrible time. Forcing myself to record gratitudes each day helped me to focus on the good things in my life rather than fixating on the bad as I had been doing of late.

I think documenting my gratitudes also helped me be more present, knowing that I was going to have to write down five things each day. Between that and my daily meditation, I can honestly say that after a few weeks, I was feeling different. I was able to remain calmer and more focused, and was actually starting to like myself again.

6
Finding Boundaries

At this lowest point of my life, I was desperately missing Teresa, who would have been so comforting to me through all of this. I had also taken a break from my counseling sessions to give me time to practice meditation, be more present, and start to process everything. I found myself feeling at a loss for how to start moving forward other than what I was already doing.

Then I got the answer, probably because I had started to still my mind enough to be present. For twenty-five years I had made the bed each morning with my husband. Routinely we threw a decorative pillow up on the bed, not thinking twice about it. But for some reason this particular morning, I actually stopped and really examined the pillow. The stitching spelled out the first verse of the Serenity Prayer, the common name for a prayer written by Reinhold Niebuhr, an American theologian, which reads:

God grant me the serenity
To accept the things I cannot change;

Courage to change the things I can;
And wisdom to know the difference.

Living one day at a time;
Enjoying one moment at a time;
Accepting hardships as the pathway to peace;
Taking, as He did, this sinful world
As it is, not as I would have it;
Trusting that He will make all things right
If I surrender to His Will;
So that I may be reasonably happy in this life
And supremely happy with Him
Forever and ever in the next. Amen.

Aside from times in desperation and Bible study groups, how often do we actually think about the meaning of the words in this or any other prayer? It is just like anything else. We do not take time to intentionally reflect.

When I took the time that morning to break down the actual meaning of the Serenity Prayer, I realized it was a simple prayer of hope for direction when one does not know which way to turn. It is no wonder why recovery networks like Alcoholics Anonymous (AA) and Narcotics Anonymous (NA) have adopted it.

Here I was grasping for some direction, and thankfully I reflected on the pillow that morning. I decided it was time for me to put the Serenity Prayer into action in my life. By intentionally evaluating what I *can* change as well as what I *cannot*, everything became much clearer and more manageable.

PART THREE

Spending Time and

Energy Where It Matters

7
Plan for Action

I anxiously sat down to sort through how I could move on from this overwhelming sadness I was feeling. Basically, I put the Serenity Prayer into action with three simple steps:

1. I listed my **PROBLEMS** that were keeping me from serenity.
2. I listed the associated things that **I CAN CHANGE** and those **I CANNOT CHANGE.**
3. I listed the associated **ACTIONS** I would take for each change to bring me closer to serenity.

Acting on the Loss of My Friend

It was impossible for me to ever bring Teresa back, so I had no other choice but to begin to accept her death. I started the process by making my prayers and meditation intentions very specific with the inclusion of "Grant me the serenity to accept Teresa's death."

Next, I approached her husband about the idea of me being Myra's mentor of the arts, one of the many things that had bonded Teresa and me. He was thrilled with the offer! Since my sons were grown and I had been away from activities appropriate for her age group for some time, I began by researching what was available for three-year-olds in our area. There were many options, and Myra and I began to do something together every few weeks.

Other than the normal sorrow associated with the death of someone you love, there was something else that bothered me after Teresa's passing—the fact that it was not until after she died that I actually had the defining moment that she was a best friend of mine. At that point it was too late to tell her and show her, but it really made me start thinking about all the relationships with people in my life.

I began to do a lot of research into the area of relationships and friendships. Somehow or other, I wanted to find a way to ensure that I and others intentionally thought about the people in our lives so that we were mindfully spending time and efforts with the people who mattered most.

Problem(s)

The loss of my friend

Change(s)

I CANNOT	BUT	I CAN

- Bring Teresa back

- Try to expose Myra to arts and entertainment enjoyed by her mother and me
- Consciously reflect on the relationships I have with the people in my life

Action(s) I Will Take

- Pray for help in acceptance
- Set "acceptance for serenity" as meditation intention

- Get agreement from Myra's dad to be her arts and entertainment mentor
- Schedule regular art project and show outings every few weeks with Myra
- Develop a way to assess relationships
- Assess myself as a friend
- Treat and allocate my time according to assessment findings
- Share this lesson and tool with others

Acting on the Loss of My Career

While it was a blessing in disguise for my "release" from the company, being "rejected" still hurt. When I talked to my counselor about how I could get past this nagging and hurtful feeling, she gave me an interesting and challenging homework assignment. In as much detail as I could imagine, she had me write a description of how I saw my life five years from that day. This was to include where I saw myself living, what my typical week was like, who was around me, what I was earning, what I looked and dressed like, etc.

She would ask questions about it each week, getting at things I had not even thought about including in my description. In the end, I was able to visualize myself in my next career, still happily married to my husband, in good shape with a soft and casual look, enjoying travel both business-related and strictly personal, and hopefully being close by to my sons and their newly formed families.

We left off with her telling me to go off and start taking the steps to make it happen, and call her as needed. This book is one of the steps toward making that vision a reality. I review the vision each month and in depth each year as part of my annual birthday self-reflection. I make adjustments as necessary, but I am pretty much staying the course. It is helpful to be able to visualize where you want to be.

I have not missed my former workplace at all. I am appreciative of the skills I acquired over the years. They have served me well to help others and myself as I evolve into my new career. It took a while, but I finally have my confidence back and like myself again, and I attribute it to my new serenity mindset that is helped by my daily reflections, meditation, and my being out of a toxic work environment.

Problem(s)

The loss of my career

Change(s)

I CANNOT	BUT	I CAN
• Change the fact that I was part of a resource action		• Change my mindset from being laid off to having the opportunity to do something new

Action(s) I Will Take

• Pray for help with feeling of rejection • Take advantage of educational and job search services	• Participate in weekly counseling sessions • Document vision of life five years from now • Review progress toward vision monthly • Wean from weekly counseling sessions

Acting on the Loss of My Husband

At the onset, I did not know if there was another woman in the picture or not, but even if there was, I was not going to lose hope, and therefore just wanted to slow things down. One morning, the quote and message in my daily SpiritJava by Gregg Kennard, the founder and senior leader of the Atlanta NSPIRE Outreach, read:

> *We make our decisions, and then our decisions turn around and make us.*
>
> — *F. W. Boreham*

> *It is important to never make a major, long-term decision from a place of emotion. Feelings are temporary and cannot be trusted . . . they change like weather patterns. Certainly we should feel and experience our emotions, as they are part of our humanity. But we should avoid decision making during extreme times of anger, sadness, loneliness, attraction, frustration, etc.*

This really resonated with my concern about slowing things down, so I sent it to Lew with a note encouraging him to take as long as he needed to sort through things. This was a huge step on my part, as I had not been a proponent of separation before now.

Next I wrote him a letter of apology for how hateful I had been, and for how I had just expected that he would tolerate me regardless of my behavior. I confessed that while I could not erase the past, I would not take him for granted, nor let another day go by in my lifetime without him knowing how much he meant to me.

For the next forty days, I made it a point to let him know how much I loved him through cards, little gifts, cookies, calls, simple notes, etc. I had hoped he would come around at the end of that time, just like major transformations occurred in the Bible in forty days. But I would have to wait longer. On the fifty-second day, he said that he was thinking about moving back in because if we were going to work things out, we needed to be together. While exciting, it was also a bit awkward at first.

We were going for weekly marriage counseling sessions, and learning things about communications that, sadly, everyone should have learned much earlier in their lives. I was still letting Lew know how important he was to me on a daily basis, and even started to bring him a weekly red rose for his desk beginning on the sixty-ninth day. He still gets those weekly roses now!

During this time, I was also attending my mindfulness-based stress reduction class. The practice of stilling myself, setting daily intentions, and meditating helped me immensely through this time of marriage limbo. It was now nearly seven months since Lew initially left, and I was still waiting for him to decide whether or not he still wanted to be married to me. I can still recall his look when I told the marriage counselor that "It is a weird feeling for me because I do not feel like I am really married, but I am not really single either."

Problem(s)

The loss of my husband

Change(s)

I CANNOT	BUT	I CAN
• Stop him from leaving		• Change mindset from being rejected by husband to not giving up on "us"

Action(s) I Will Take

• Pray for strength, courage, and guidance • Practice regular meditation to calm mind	• Let go of imagined scenarios, e.g., another woman, never coming back, etc. • Show him how much I care about him • Focus on how I want things to be versus how they are at the moment

8
Perseverance Pays Off

Sometime during my trifecta-of-losses period, I found a quote that I kept close by as a reminder for the need to be patient:

> *In the confrontation between the stream and the rock, the stream always wins, not through strength but with perseverance.* (H. Jackson Brown Jr., author of *Life's Little Instruction Book*)

With this in mind, I compassionately put my time and effort into the things that I could change and make a difference in, and away from dwelling on circumstances that I could not change.

Finding Serenity in the Loss of Teresa

I made Myra and her dad a bigger part of my life to help them along, and started to mentor Myra through outings every few weeks. Whether it was an art project, a show, a festival, a sleepover, or just having a picnic and collecting things in nature, we enjoyed each other's company. She is now elementary school age. As time goes on and we spend more time together, she says and does so many things just like her mom that at times, I feel like I am with a mini Teresa.

Close to a year after Teresa's death, her ashes were buried at a beautiful natural cemetery, with a very intimate and touching memorial service. For many months I had a difficult time processing and believing that Teresa was gone. That day I finally felt acceptance.

As for the development of a way to proactively reflect on relationships, part four of this book outlines the technique I designed and tested to evaluate the relationships in our lives, so that we can be sure we are spending our time with the people who matter in terms of our overall well-being.

Those who have used the relationship assessment tool have been surprised with some of the results, but their reactions have been consistent: "I am surprised that some people ended up where they did, but now I can see why . . . this is an interesting and eye-opening self-assessment of my relationships that will really help me prioritize my time and efforts with the right people."

Finding Serenity in the Loss of My Career

In job interviews, I recall being asked the question "Where do you want to be five years from now?" but I never gave it enough thought to actually be able to visualize myself in a place doing something in particular. That is, until now, when I got the homework assignment of documenting what my life would look like in five years.

To even take my first stab at this vision of myself was tough. And then every time I thought I had described my five-year view in all the detail I could imagine, my counselor would pose devil's advocate questions about it, and I would find myself back working on the next version of it. After perhaps five versions, she asked me one last question—"What is keeping you from starting to work toward this vision?" The only legitimate answer I had was that I had not seen the vision until now.

So off I went to start working on it. We were able to reduce my weekly counseling sessions to monthly at first, where we would review my progress toward the vision. After a few months, I decided I could manage the monthly reviews on my own, and I continue to do that on the first Friday of each month.

Finding Serenity in the Loss of My Husband

My meditation teachings and practice helped me to put the imagined scenarios and what-ifs out of my head. This allowed me to put my mind and energy on what was most important to me—getting "us" back again.

I started each day with a positive intention of letting go of the idea that there was someone else in his life, and focusing instead on words and actions that would show him how much I loved him and wanted him back. I made a pact to myself that never again would I not reinforce how important Lew is to me on a daily basis.

As I mentioned, throughout our separation, we were seeing a marriage counselor who taught us things about communications that everyone should learn much earlier in their lives, and at a minimum before getting married! This helped us tremendously to see that much of our bickering was a result of communications. Things improved to the point that we spread our counseling sessions more weeks apart from each other.

Lew eventually moved back to the house, recognizing that in order to really work on this, we needed to be living together and not just "dating." Everyday living was going well; when we were bothered by something, we used the communication tools we learned at counseling to work through things. We even took some weekend trips together, and those as well were great.

Lew suggested we get away one Friday to the mountains, and just go up to the mountains and have a burger and beer at the place by the river that we had enjoyed many years ago. I'm a sucker for going up to the mountains any time of the year, so I was ready and willing.

Little did I know that he had also planned to drive back home by the place we had gotten married almost twenty-six years before, and ask me if I wanted to recommit to our marriage! I said yes, so we walked over to the garden area where we first made our vows. For some reason he was reluctant to "trespass," but I insisted it had to be in the same spot. He, our beloved dog Zorro, and I were standing right where we recited our initial vows. There were a couple of people scurrying about close by. As they got closer, I could see that it was my neighbor friend, Marcy, and my younger sister, Elaine. My husband had arranged for them to be our witnesses. They took pictures of us, and then the gardener took pictures of all of us.

I was shocked and speechless . . . Lew had completely caught me off guard. He had every detail covered! I was so happy not only with the surprise, but by the fact that we were really married again after nearly a year of limbo.

The surprise did not stop up in the mountains. On our way home I suggested that we get in touch with our sons and all go out to dinner to celebrate. Unannounced to me, Lew had already been in communication with them, and they were aware of this whole recommitment plan! In fact, one of them had picked up my sister at the airport early that morning and brought her to Marcy's house.

Lew said that our sons would be coming over later to celebrate, along with the other people he had invited to stop by. He had handpicked the guests to not only help celebrate with us, but also to thank them for their support through this life-changing journey.

A caterer showed up with food, my husband opened wine and beer, and people started coming in one by one. Each of them had played a special role over this past year and a half, starting with Teresa's passing until now. What a delightful and unforgettable surprise!

As difficult and hard as the past eighteen months had been, it resulted in our marriage reaching a very different level. We now consciously show each other appreciation and do not take for granted that we are not only spouses, but the very best of friends as well. We communicate openly, listening to each other's perspectives, and recognizing and respecting that what is said is not necessarily what is always heard. We also pay careful attention to how we allocate our time, having learned that we were spending too much time with other people and not enough time with each other.

What a beautiful ending and new beginning!

9
Serenity Steps Approach to Gain Clarity

There was a time when I wondered if, after all the trials I had gone through, I would ever get to a point of being able to be grateful and thankful for the pain that I experienced. You know that whole thing about "things happen for a reason." So what, pray tell, was the lesson I learned after losing my dear friend, my career/identity, and my husband?

> Be thankful for your trials. If you're being tested, you're being perfected. Which means you have a divine purpose and reason to rejoice.
> –Author Unknown

I was fortunate enough to learn multiple lessons, for which I share techniques for achieving in this book. Two of the lessons are (1) to still my mind in order to move forward and end up whole; and (2) to set boundaries by accepting what I can and cannot change.

During my difficult time, I learned the importance of beginning each day by stilling my mind. I began a morning ritual then that I continue to practice most mornings even now. I start the day with my "tranquility trio":

1. **Meditation**—ten to forty-five minutes depending on what is going on in my life
2. **Prayer**—I express my thanks and re-member all of those in need, including specific people on my list
3. **Reflection**—a combination of journaling what is on my mind, listing five gratitudes, and setting a daily intention

Without this daily practice, who knows if I would have been still enough to take to heart the message that fate (God) unveiled to me that one morning on the Serenity Prayer pillow. It was through that intervention that I got the revelation to literally break down the prayer into the **Serenity Steps Approach**.

Intentionally thinking about what you can and cannot control and change results in setting boundaries that truly simplify your life and keep your focus on the things that matter.

What has been so amazing to me is the amount of unnecessary worry and fear and concern I have removed from my life by just thinking through these three simple steps. They work really well on the smallest everyday situations as well by serving as a simple framework for solving problems.

Let's use a couple of simple problems to demonstrate, keeping in mind that actions will vary depending on each individual situation . . .

<u>Problem Example 1</u>

There was road construction going on outside of my neighborhood on a major traffic artery. The project was going to affect commuters for two years. During this time, our neighborhood had become a cut-through for traffic, which was bad enough, but the bigger problem was that the cars were speeding through the neighborhood. This put the many bike riders, walkers, joggers, and pets at risk.

Problem(s)

The traffic speeding through the neighborhood caused a dangerous situation

Change(s)

I CANNOT	BUT	I CAN
• Mandate no cutting through • Install traffic lights or speed humps in short term		• Make the county aware of the new problem and what options they can help with for reinforcement

Action(s) I Will Take

• Warn the neighborhood to take extra precautions for safety • Make the neighborhood aware we are working on finding a resolution	• Discuss the situation with the county commissioner for our district • Per his request, send e-mail to his office requesting police patrol and any other options they have • Contact the county police department to ask for random patrolling during rush hours in the morning and early evening on cut-through streets

Do you see how helpful it is to break down which changes are doable and which ones are not? Both may require associated actions, but the decision making and next steps become very straightforward. There is no need to keep unnecessary anxiety in your life. Putting the Serenity Prayer in action works for any situation!

I was thrilled to say that within twenty-four hours of sending the e-mail to the county commissioner's office, I was doing my early morning walk and heard a siren pulling over a violator!

Problem Example 2

Many women I know are becoming empty nesters with the last of their children going off to college. It is interesting to see the gamut of emotions of these people, ranging from sheer joy to a questioning of identity. For those experiencing sheer joy, the **Serenity Steps Approach** is not necessary, as enjoyment should be simple.

But for those at the other end of the spectrum, whose role as mom has now changed and is less defined, let's look at how this approach can truly help . . .

Problem(s)

My children have grown and left "the nest," and I don't know what my new role is at home

Change(s)

I CANNOT	BUT	I CAN
• Change their age and keep them at home forever		• Request a mutual plan for regular communication • Do reasonably numbered acts of love

Action(s) I Will Take

• Pray for help in acceptance
• Set "acceptance for serenity" as meditation intention

• Explain how difficult the transition of them being away is for you, and how it would help if you had regular catch-up times
• Come to agreement on something that works for both of you and is not too imposing on him/her

• Send thinking of you card, text, photo, token gift
• As appropriate, plan short visit and dinner

• Connect regularly as agreed, and make the communication enjoyable and informative for both of you

Change(s)

| I CANNOT | BUT | I CAN |

- Stifle their independence and path to spreading their own wings

- Consciously determine if plan needs to be altered
- Use this empty-nest opportunity to get to know my spouse again (if applicable)

Action(s) I Will Take

- Be proud you raised them to be independent and to survive on their own
- Encourage them to continue to grow and experience new things while using care and common sense
- Reinforce your support and availability whenever they might need it

- Tell him/her you want to chat about it so to think about what they would like to change about communication plan
- Set aside a specific time to have discussions
- Modify as needed or continue to enjoy status quo
- Explain how difficult the empty-nest transition is for you and how it would help if he/she understood that situation
- Propose that the two of you start getting to know each other again now that the distractions associated with raising children are gone
- Set aside some of the time you used to spend with the children to do something together regularly

Hopefully these examples demonstrate how helpful this approach can be to logically thinking through problems, regardless of the magnitude, and getting you to focus on actions that make a difference rather than worrying about the things you cannot control.

The Importance of Stilling the Mind

I cannot emphasize enough the benefit of stilling the mind, even if for a short time each day. While many people say they cannot be still or are too busy, keep in mind the words of the late American motivational speaker and author Zig Ziglar who clarified such excuses by saying that "Lack of direction, not lack of time, is the problem. We all have twenty-four-hour days."

It is easy to get caught up in the crazy pace of the world these days. When I was in the corporate world, I was intrigued by meditation, especially when learning how many extremely successful people practice it. You see the same success in people who practice prayer regularly. But I did not make time to learn about it, or do it, because I was "too busy."

There is an old Zen proverb that summarizes the ironic fallacy in this modern-day thinking:

*If you don't have time to meditate for fifteen
minutes . . .
Then you need to meditate for an hour!*

Had I known then how much taking time for stillness sharpens focus and increases productivity, I would have made time to start practicing stillness much sooner. There is even medical proof that if one takes the time to just stop and still oneself while breathing, meditating, and/or praying, a person is able to calm and cope with the stresses of life more effectively.

The results for me have been so beneficial that it has been part of my daily practice now for several years. Not only do I attribute my Serenity Prayer revelation to finally stilling my mind, but those who knew me from before also recognize me as a calmer person now. I think the benefits are best described by the following published by the World Fellowship of Buddhists in *World Buddhism, Volume 22*, in 1973:

> *It may be stating the case too strongly to say
> that in meditation one seeks to gain nothing.
> For there is an increase in happiness and peace
> of mind. But when asked, "What have you
> gained from meditation?" the answer would
> be: "It is not what I have gained that is important*

*but rather what I have diminished, namely,
greed, hatred, and delusion."*

I cannot tell you what to think, act, or feel, but I do hope that you will at least try the **Serenity Steps Approach** the next time you are at a loss for which way to turn and in need of clarity and direction. Since realizing this technique, it seems I often find myself in the company of someone who is talking about something that has them very distraught. After talking to them about what they can and cannot change about the situation, and then discussing the possible associated action steps, the relief on their faces at the end of the discussion is priceless!

PART FOUR

Surrounding Yourself with Meaningful Relationships

10
Everybody Isn't Your Friend

Remember how I had made a note to myself after Teresa's death to explore my relationships in greater detail once I got to a point where my head was clearer? I did not want a repeat of being too late to recognize how important someone was in my life, nor did I want anyone else to feel this painful regret.

With my mind more still at this point, I was determined to find a way to ensure that I and others were very much aware of the people with whom we should be spending more of our time and efforts.

I came across a poem by an unknown author, about how people come and go in our lives for a reason, a season, or a lifetime . . .

A Reason, A Season, or A Lifetime
—Author Unknown

People come into your life for a reason, a season, or a lifetime.

When you figure out which one it is,
you will know what to do for each person.
When someone is in your life for a REASON,
it is usually to meet a need you have expressed.
They have come to assist you through a difficulty;
to provide you with guidance and support;
to aid you physically, emotionally, or spiritually.
They may seem like a godsend, and they are.
They are there for the reason you need them to be.

Then, without any wrongdoing on your part
or at an inconvenient time,
this person will say or do something to bring
the relationship to an end.
Sometimes they die. Sometimes they walk away.
Sometimes they act up and force you to take a stand.
What we must realize is that our need has been
met, our desire fulfilled; their work is done.
The prayer you sent up has been answered and
now it is time to move on.

Some people come into your life for a SEASON,
because your turn has come to share, grow or learn.
They bring you an experience of peace or make
you laugh.
They may teach you something you have never
done.

*They usually give you an unbelievable amount
of joy.
Believe it. It is real. But only for a season.*

*LIFETIME relationships teach you lifetime lessons;
things you must build upon in order to have a
solid emotional foundation.
Your job is to accept the lesson, love the person,
and put what you have learned to use in all
other relationships and areas of your life.
It is said that love is blind but friendship is
clairvoyant.*

Two things resonated with me when reading this:

1. As is the nature of life, friendships and
    relationships will eventually come to
    an end.
2. It helps to focus on what you have learned
    or how you have grown from your
    relationships, instead of on the loss.

Having learned many lifelong lessons from both
my friend Teresa and my husband Lew, it really did
help when I shifted my focus to those things rather
than them being gone. Actually, reflecting on some of
the lessons even brought some smiles to my saddened

face. This refocus also made me very appreciative of the comfort and things I was learning from those who were there to support me in one way or another during this difficult time in my life.

At the same time, it made me stop and think about all of the people in my life, and honestly, I found myself confused about many things concerning my relationships . . .

- Why did I not have the defining moment that Teresa was a best friend until it was too late?
- Why did I not hear from any recent work colleagues when I got laid off?
- Why did I not realize that losing my husband also meant that I would be losing my number-one best friend?
- Why was I so surprised by who was there to show support versus who wasn't in my time of need?

I was very interested in getting underneath these questions. This is when I came across a quote by Trent Shelton that reads:

> *Everybody isn't your friend. Just because they hang around you and laugh with you doesn't mean they're for you. Just because they say they*

got your back, doesn't mean they won't stab
you in it. People pretend well. Jealousy sometimes
doesn't live far. So know your circle. At the end
of the day, real situations expose fake people so
pay attention.

It was time for me to "know my circle." Obviously there were those I socialized with, and there were those with whom I could talk about things that I would never discuss with many others. Some of those in my circle lived nearby, while others were thousands of miles away. But what was it that really made them different from each other? Which ones were my genuine friends?

11
Meaningful Relationships Are Key to Overall Well-Being

As a market researcher by profession, I began digging into everything I could find related to friendships and relationships. I was shocked at the number of well-conducted research studies that had been done in the area of relationships, many with findings that clearly showed that the same level of risk as many other well-known health factors was posed by not creating and maintaining quality close relationships.

Loneliness and lack of social relationships are:

- Equivalent to smoking fifteen cigarettes a day[2]
- Equivalent to being an alcoholic[2]
- More harmful than not exercising[2]
- Twice as harmful as obesity[2]
- Increasing your odds of developing dementia by 64 percent[3]
- Increasing your odds of premature death by 14 percent[4]

Not a day goes by when we don't hear from media, medical, and well-being professionals about eating right,

The influence of social relationships on risk for mortality is comparable with well-established risk factors for mortality.[2]

exercising, getting enough sleep—the list goes on and on. Why were we not hearing the same kind of encouragement to focus on meaningful relationships? It seems to be largely missing from both our conversations and media focus regarding health.

In their book *The Lonely American: Drifting Apart in the Twenty-first Century*, Jacqueline Olds, MD, and Richard S. Schwartz, MD, discussed the research they did to understand this often avoided topic in America—loneliness, which seems to be a repercussion of our frenzied lifestyles today.

They stated that social support is an important and independent determinant of overall health, with significant effects on longevity, on response to stress, on the robustness of immune functions, and on the incidence and course of a variety of specific illnesses.

But do you want to hear an incredible finding they quoted out of a report from the 2003 Dahlem Workshop on Attachment and Bonding that succinctly summarizes a much larger research effort?

Positive social relationships are second only to genetics in predicting health and longevity in humans.[5]

This is a sobering fact that puts a whole different perspective on what is important for our overall well-being and longevity. If you think about it, though, this should come as no surprise. Let's face it: people need people. We are social creatures by nature and are truly not designed to live in social isolation. For much of human history, people resided in small hunter-gatherer communities. In fact, forming small groups to address any situation has been the survival strategy of the human species. Isolation is devastating to the human psyche, which is why solitary confinement is considered the cruelest of punishments.

Are We Not at Risk?

I figured that perhaps the reason we are not hearing about the importance of social relationships is because, in the whole scheme of things, we do not have an isolation problem. That was my wishful thinking until I came across a study that compared data from the General Social Survey (GSS), one of the nation's longest-running surveys of social, cultural, and political issues.

Additional questions were added to a standard set of questions for special studies. The last confidant-related survey was done in 1985, and the questions were repeated in 2004 to measure how people's social networks had changed over time. The question that was asked in both surveys that led to a very telling trend was, *From time to time, people discuss important matters with other people. Can you tell me in the last six months who you've discussed important matters with?*

Analysis of the data showed that in the twenty-year period from the time the study was first done to when it was redone, the number of confidants claimed on average by Americans dropped from almost three to two, and the number of people who said they had no one with whom to discuss important matters more than doubled to nearly 25 percent.[6] Bottom line, this shows that Americans' circle of close confidants had shrunk dramatically over the two-decade period.

Why the Big Change?

Why are our circles of genuine friends shrinking? We do not know for sure, but one can point to numerous factors that can potentially lead to this decline. Perhaps meaningful relationships have been replaced by screens and gadgets? Maybe it is longer work hours, longer commutes, family demands and responsibilities, or the sheer increased demands of our 24/7 lives? Or is it that people have become more transient, or that many towns have grown to a size where there is no longer the feeling of belonging to a village?

According to research, humans have difficulty resisting rewards that arrive at unpredictable time intervals, making such rewards addictive. Social network notifications and slot machines share this trait! So maybe social media keeping us addicted to "busy-ness" and self-involvement has taken the place of genuine communication with friends?

Whatever the reason may be, we assume greater health and well-being risks if we do not make time for meaningful relationships.

Are All Relationships Beneficial to Overall Well-Being?

Please do not think for a moment that if you have lots of Facebook friends that you do not have to worry about increased risks to your overall health and well-being. Nothing could be further from the truth!

In fact, I want to be very clear about something. The meaningful associations that contribute to overall well-being are **NOT** to be confused with the many, very loosely connected relationships we all have in our lives. The term "friend" has become so loosely used that it undermines how very special such a bond is. Merriam-Webster offers that not only is there a strong liking between friends, but there is also trust. That is very different than the relationship you have online with someone you may barely even know. A good test of your genuine friends is who you hear from on your birthday without the help of Facebook.

friend
noun \ 'frend \
Definition of friend

1. a person who has a strong liking for and trust in another person
2. a person who is not an enemy *<friend or foe>*
3. a person who helps or supports something *<She was a friend to environmental causes.>*

While technology may be partially to blame as a result of social media labeling the numerous contacts associated with you as "friends," not a day passes when I do not hear someone relay a story about something that involved a "friend of theirs." If you probe much about the "friend," you find that the two barely know each other. What ever happened to saying "someone I know" instead of making the leap to "a friend of mine"?

To demonstrate the huge difference, just close your eyes for a minute. Take a deep breath or two to relax. Now reflect back to a particular pleasant memory in your life . . . it can be of an event, a specific person, etc. Picture where you were, who you were with, what you were doing, what you were wearing, and so on. Enjoy reminiscing for a bit and then open your eyes.

It is very likely you were not alone in the memory you chose. There is a good chance that the people you were with are an example of the close ties the research refers to as being beneficial to your health, happiness, and overall well-being. These are the genuine friends and family with whom you have close, secure, and supportive relationships. They are the ones with whom we experience both positive and negative emotions, and with whom we are able to talk openly and feel listened to and understood. They give and receive support; it is not a one-way relationship. And we make time with them to have fun and share new experiences that ultimately lead to future fond memories like the one about which you just reminisced.

Different Types of Relationships

While there are many nomenclatures to group the various types of relationships, I found that four categories work for clear differentiation: (1) Acquaintances, (2) Casual Friends, (3) True Friends, and (4) Best Friends.

Acquaintances

This is the type of relationship we have with people when we initially meet them. We are very guarded rather than open, and without knowing the person, it makes both empathy and connection very limited. Often these relationships are viewed as too temporary to be worth the effort.

The way people become acquainted is normally through a common venue, e.g., same neighborhood, same classrooms or teams of kids, work colleagues, chatting at a bar, fellow students in a class, club members, etc. We do not necessarily know all the people in a venue. The Acquaintances are the ones with whom you regularly exchange polite greetings.

If and when the association with the particular venue where the Acquaintance was made ends, the frequency of you seeing these people likely lessens. You may still exchange greetings if you see them at the grocery store, for example, or while waiting for a conference call to begin. While many relationships never go beyond this point, some will evolve.

By definition, an Acquaintance is *someone recognized by sight or someone known, though less intimately than a friend.*

Casual Friends

Casual Friends are Acquaintances whom we have gotten to know a bit more. The exchange of greetings has evolved to general small talk, which is easy because you have obviously met in a venue that indicates a common interest, activity, or concern. While the general small talk you have with Casual Friends likely starts with your common theme, you may begin to share more information about yourselves as well.

Think of walking into a roomful of people, many of whom you do not know. Suddenly you feel a sigh of relief when you see a face that you recognize, or hear a recognizable voice among a group of strangers on a phone call. These are the Casual Friends in contrast to the acquaintances.

Generally, you enjoy being with Casual Friends, and they are convenient to organize as a group, knowing that everyone will have something in common and get along. While great to socialize with, conversations with Casual Friends have a tendency to be fairly shallow. The only way friendships grow from this point is if there is a reciprocal interest to keep getting to know each other in greater depth.

True Friends

True friendship is more intensified because you both have had the desire and have taken the time to get to know each other much better. Conversations have more depth, sharing personal opinions and beliefs, as well as life goals.

The focus of the relationship shifts from "self" to "other," with a two-way effort to coach each other through ups and downs, and a commitment to support each other to reach life goals. True Friends enjoy the excitement and sharing of new experiences and form a history together.

As True Friends, your uncertainty about each other has been reduced to the point that you are capable of pretty much predicting each other's responses with accuracy. You can also read each other's nonverbal signs for the most part, to use as guides on when to avoid certain topics or when to console, for instance.

You view these friends as important in your life, so when conflict occurs, both of you view it as important to work through the problem, which is done through compromise and empathy, and not through nondiscussion or stand-off disagreement.

Best Friends

Best friendship is a very special bond and is something that is rarely achieved. In general, people do not like to make themselves vulnerable, but this is the unique trait of Best Friends.

Best Friends let down all walls and take the risk to share values, feelings, and confessions that may at times require courage and vulnerability to discuss. This is what formed the bond . . . the fact that they took the chance to get beyond any pretenses to reveal deep-seeded truths about themselves with each other.

Best Friends choose to unlock and share their true inner selves, epitomizing trust and respect. They commit to prioritize to openly and honestly help each other achieve an even deeper understanding of self.

Best Friends are continuously on each other's minds. They energize each other, will always make themselves available, and can make each other laugh without even trying. When Best Friends lose each other through death, or some other unforeseen closure, the pain is very deep.

Relationship Development Continuum

The different types of relationships do build on each other, but some never move beyond a certain point. Hopefully this visual (next page) helps to demonstrate that there are specific requirements, which, if unmet, prevent the relationship from further growing.

What Kind of Relationships Do I Have?

So which of these categories was the relationship I had with Teresa in? What about that with my work colleagues? And my husband? What about all those wonderful people who provided me support during my challenging time? And lastly, what about all of those people I expected to hear from in this time of need, but did not?

I suspected if I figured out a way to evaluate each of my relationships, I would find serenity from all the confusion I was feeling. Furthermore, it would help me with my interactions with various people, and perhaps be useful to other people like me as well.

Acquaintances   Casual Friends   True Friends   Best Friends

I initiated a conversation with a person whom I had been sitting next to week after week in a class. While we went on to become Casual Friends and share a common interest, the relationship will never move to true friendship because there is not a two-way commitment to put in the time to make that happen.

A Casual Friend recently went out of her way to do something to show me compassion for something that had upset me. She risked showing her beliefs with her actions, but also initiated the desire and willingness to spend time to get to know each other better.

A True Friend went through a very difficult time in her life. In my efforts to help, we let down walls and talked about things that others rarely discuss. This relationship has the potential to grow to a best friendship with more time and reciprocation.

Best Friends unlock and share their true inner selves, and prioritize open and honest help to each other to achieve deep understanding of self. Therefore, when Best Friends lose each other through death, or some other unforeseen closure, the pain is very deep.

12
Evaluating Relationships

While I have provided descriptions of the four different kinds of relationships in life, this poem called "Life is Like a Train Ride" (Author Unknown) helps bring them to mind visually . . .

Life is like a train ride.

The passengers on the train are seemingly going to the same destination as you, but based on their belief in you or their belief that the train will get them to their desired destination they will stay on the ride or they will get off somewhere during the trip.

People can and will get off at any stop.

Just know that where people get off is more of a reflection on them, than it is on you.

There will be a few people in your life that will make the whole trip with you, who believe in you, accept that you are human and that mistakes will be made along the way, and that you will get to your desired destination—together, no matter what.

Be very grateful of these people.

They are rare and when you find one, don't let go of them—ever.

Be blessed for the ones who get on at the worst stops when no one is there.

Remember those people, they are special.

Always hold them dear to your heart.

Be very wary of people sneaking on at certain stops when things are going good and acting like they have been there for the whole ride.

For they will be the first to depart.

There will be ones who secretly try to get off the ride and there will be those that very publicly will jump off.

Don't pay any heed to the defectors.

Pay heed to the passengers that are still on the trip.

They are the important ones.

If someone tries to get back on the train — don't be angry or hold a grudge, let them.

Just see where they are around the next hard turn.

If they are buckled in — accept them.

If they are pulling the hand-rail alarm again — then let them off the train freely and waste no space in your head for them again, ever.

There will be times that the train will be moving slow, at almost a crawl's pace.

Appreciate that you can take in the view.

There will be times where the train is going so fast that everything is a blur.

Enjoy the sense of speed in your life, as it is exhilarating but unsustainable.

There will also be the chance that the train derails.

If that does happen, it will hurt, a lot, for a long time.

But there will be people who will appear out of nowhere who will get you back on track.

Those will be the people that will matter most in your life.

Love them forever.

For you can never repay these people.

The thing is, that even if you could repay them, they wouldn't accept it anyway.

Just pay it forward.

Eventually your train will get to its final stop and you will need to deboard.

At that time you will realize that life is about the journey AND the destination.

Know and have faith that at the end of your ride your train will have the right passengers on board and all the passengers that were on board at one time or another were there for a distinct purpose.

Enjoy the ride.

It offers a nice visualization of the friendships you want to cherish, versus those on which you probably do not want to spend much time. In reading the poem, I compared the passengers on the train to my relationships, thinking there may be some correlation that might explain my surprise of who was and who was not there for support during my difficult time.

Who was making the whole trip with me? Who got on at the worst stops to be there for me? Who appeared out of nowhere to get me back on track? And who was jumping on and off the train?

Reviewing My Relationships

I started by putting together a list of all relationships in my life, including family, friends, neighbors, work colleagues, hobby buddies, parents of my sons' friends, etc. This became like a walk down memory lane as I thought of many people who had played a part in my life, but with whom I no longer kept in touch! I realized that in order to make this most useful, I would limit this **Relationship Inventory** to those that were more "active," i.e., those with whom I was in touch at least once a year.

While this requires some time to put together, it is a very interesting exercise. It is also not anything I would have to create from scratch again if I were to repeat this evaluation in the future. At that point, all I would have to do is simply add any new relationships and/or delete those that were no longer active in my life.

When I finished my list, it was immediately apparent that there were varying degrees of closeness between the people recorded and me. A handful were those who knew all about me, and I knew all about them. Others were more acquaintances, with whom I had only very surface-level relationships. And then there were many that were somewhere in between.

Being a visual person, I pictured this list of people fitting into a group of concentric rings. The definition of "concentric" is *having a common center,* so I put myself in the center ring, with four other rings of relationships around me, varying by their level of closeness.

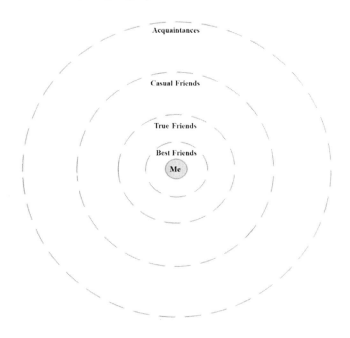

Now I needed a consistent way of positioning each person on my list to the appropriate relationship ring. This is where my background as a market researcher became very beneficial. Not only did it help me sort through all of the information I had found on relationships, but based on my experience, I was able to develop a relationship assessment and scoring algorithm based on key traits and the development continuum of relationships.

Having developed many assessment tools over the course of my career, I felt comfortable with the survey and how it worked in plotting my own relationships. Knowing it was important to test this tool with other people, I solicited dozens of people to go through the process of listing their relationships and responding to the **Relationship Assessment Survey** for each person. Their feedback enabled me to (1) improve the survey questions; (2) have confidence the survey worked; and (3) create an Internet-based tool to automate the process. Ironically each one of the testers had the same reaction, admitting that while there were some surprises in which ring some people landed, the positioning actually made sense and would help them as they allocated their time among relationships moving forward. A copy of the assessment survey questions can be found in **Tools and Resources** at the end of this book.

Placement on the Relationship Compass

A picture is always worth a thousand words, and this is no exception. Once the rings are populated with the relationship names, the importance of each becomes very clear.

Notice how the rings are bigger the farther away from the center that they are? This is based on the distribution of relationships within the rings. The number of *Best Friends* will be far fewer in number than that of *Acquaintances*, and therefore a much smaller ring.

People often ask me about the number of relationships in each ring. While not precise, on average, the breakdown might look something like this:

Best Friends	1–5	*Casual Friends*	30–40
True Friends	12–15	*Acquaintances*	100s

Where the name is placed within a ring is also differentiating. Based on the survey scoring algorithm, some people are near the edge closer to the middle, while others are near the further away edge. See www.nancymforbes.com for survey details.

Placement on this chart provided me so much clarity about the many relationship questions I had after my trying time that I came to refer to it as my **Relationship Compass**™ because of the direction it provided.

Relationship Compass

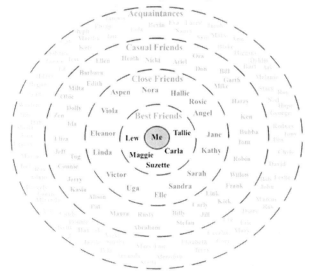

Now it is very clear that my friend Teresa would have been in the Best Friends' circle, which is why I was agonizing over her loss. My husband Lew was also a Best Friend, causing a double-edged pain of losing both my spouse and a best friend. My more recent work colleagues were predominantly Acquaintances, which explained why I was not hearing from them for support. And finally, I now knew why some people I would have expected to be around at my time of need were not; they were Casual Friends, and only enjoyed being around for the fun, socializing times together.

It was very apparent that I had been misallocating my time, from which I learned three very important lessons:

1. I was spending far too much time with casual friends, at the expense of time spent nurturing my closest friends, including my husband.
2. I was spending too little time building new relationships, which is really important because you never know when you might lose one.
3. I was letting negative energy relationships drain both my time and me.

Putting What I Learned into Action

So how do you make sure you are spending time with the people who really do contribute to your health, happiness, and overall well-being? You proactively put together an **Annual Relationship Action Plan.**

Recall that the lines forming the rings on the compass are not solid because they are designed for slow but continuous movement that occurs between them. We can go through life just letting this movement happen, or we can choose to steer it with a proactive relationship plan. Which relationships do you want to nurture? Which ones do you want to try to grow or develop? Where will you go to seek out potential new acquaintances who may develop into genuine friends? Is there anyone not on the compass with whom you would like to try to reconnect? Which relationships, if any, are draining and thus potentials to deemphasize or let go?

13
Allocating Relationship Time

Because of my lesson on how I was misallocating my time with people in the past, I designed my relationship plan for the year to achieve six complementary objectives:

1. Cherish my best friends
2. Recognize my significant other as my number-one best friend
3. Connect regularly with my true friends
4. Manage my time spent with casual friends
5. Initiate and cultivate new acquaintances
6. Deemphasize my negative-energy relationships

Specific names (WHO) from my relationship compass were associated with each of these objectives (WHAT), along with the WHEN and HOW for each. Before showing you what a sampling of my plan looks like, let's look at each objective in depth.

Cherishing My Best Friends

Best friends are very, very special. You don't get that many of these people in your life, so it is critical to cherish them. They are a blessing or a gift that we have given to ourselves through opening up our hearts to them, and they in return open up their hearts to us.

The way I cherish my best friends is to treat them the way I would want to be treated as a best friend. I now make myself very aware of who they are and let them know on a regular basis how important they are to me. I also make a point of telling them about important things in my life, so that I never risk those going unsaid like I learned the hard way with Teresa's death.

I maintain regular contact with them and show them appreciation and respect. No matter what I have going on in my life, I make time for offering support or advice when needed. As issues arise, I initiate a discussion right away, knowing they just don't go away themselves. I forgive minor wrongdoings, which are inevitable, and try to find an honest and supportive approach when it comes to concerning matters. If it is something that would benefit them, I am generous with my talents, such as decorating, gardening, cooking, and organizing. And of course, I always show up for important events, e.g., a new baby, memorials, openings, wedding, etc.

I have lots of entries on my calendar for my best friends to be sure nothing slips through the cracks. For each one of them, I have reminders for:

- Monthly (at minimum) Connections – either by phone, e-mail, text, or visit, depending on logistics
- Upcoming Important Dates – to call, text, or send note just beforehand and also to follow up as appropriate
- Birthdays (noting milestones) – to send a card and maybe a small gift, as well as call, text, or e-mail
- Annual Commitment Discussion – an in-depth discussion about our friendship (what we like or don't like, what we would like to try to change in the coming year, etc.). A guide for this discussion can be found in Tools and Resources

Additionally, I am diligent about returning phone calls, e-mails, or text messages, as well as acknowledging cards and gifts. When I am reminded of them for some reason, I send a quick text/photo with a "thinking of you" note. I also like to surprise them with random acts of kindness in the forms of small gifts, unexpected visits or hugs, surprises, or just an out-of-the-blue call.

For long-distance friendships, if possible, I try to see them at least once a year.

Does this sound like a lot of work? It requires some time but is also fun and very rewarding, making it well worth the investment. It very much is a labor of love versus work. Seriously, getting this set up on your calendar is the only really tedious part of the whole thing.

Recognizing My Significant Other as My Number-One Best Friend

Because we often spend more time with a significant other than we do with our other best friends, there is more of a tendency to take each other for granted. This is what happened in my marriage, as mentioned earlier in the book.

I will never forget a conversation I had years ago with a friend whose husband had gone through a tough fight with cancer. At times the battle was so tough she had to think about what it would be like if he did not survive. If that happened, she said that what made her most sad was the thought that "she would never again be anyone's number one!" The fighter he is, he did survive and is thriving, thank goodness.

When Lew left, I was reminded of this conversation. I realized that neither one of us had been treating each other as number one. We used to, so I knew it was possible. When we recommitted our life together, we recommitted to being each other's number one, the epitome of a best friend.

How do I now recognize my husband as my *Number-One Best Friend?* I do all the same things I do for my other best friends, but there are some really important additions:

- Demonstration of love, affection, appreciation, and respect **daily.**
- Acknowledgment through both words and behavior how much you value what they do for you.
- Do something special for each other weekly; I bring him a red rose for his desk each week.
- Communicate with each other, recognizing a very basic guideline from the book *Men Are from Mars, Women Are from Venus.* Acknowledge that many men thrive on trust and attention, while many women thrive on attention and understanding.
- Spend an evening together taking the love-language quiz from the book *The*

5 Love Languages: The Secret to Love that Lasts. Spend the next few nights cuddling and taking turns to read the book aloud together, discussing how it relates to your answers on the quiz. Once you know each other's love languages, check on how well you are doing on these at least once a year.

- Devote time and attention as during courtship. Do not have a false sense of security that because you have been together for so many years, you will always be together.
- Make each anniversary a true celebration of "us" by spending the day together. It is a great time to talk about whether or not you are happy as "us" and what, if any, changes you would like to make.

Connecting Regularly with My True Friends

While not *Best Friends*, these ties are very strong. In fact, some may become *Best Friends* over time. The biggest difference between *Best* and *True* friends is that while you are very open with *True Friends*, you have not committed to helping each other be your best selves, nor, probably, do you connect as often.

Generally speaking, while I connect with my *Best Friends* at least each month, I may only be in touch with my *True Friends* once a quarter at a minimum. Aside from this frequency of connections, I treat my *True Friends* the same as my *Best Friends* with one exception:

Earlier I mentioned the Annual Commitment Discussions I do with my best friends. I only do this with **some** *True Friends*. I listen to my heart in many of these instances. Some of these friendships are fine as they are, while others may be moving in either the direction of becoming closer, or further apart. With those that I sense are moving in either direction, I initiate an in-depth discussion about our friendship (what we like or don't like, what we would like to try to change in the coming year, etc.) I then incorporate the outcome of that discussion in my relationship action plan and work on it accordingly.

Managing Time Spent with Casual Friends

A person can easily fall into a trap with *Casual Friends*. There can be thirty to forty friends in this group, as it often includes your "go-to" people for socializing, activities, hobbies, etc. They are convenient to gather together without much notice, effort, or planning. You have fun with *Casual Friends*, but you can also get in ruts here, spending many hours in fairly shallow conversations that never seem to go anywhere. In fact, this group can have the tendency to talk over one another and not be very good listeners. Without caution, you can end up having every weekend booked on your calendar with *Casual Friends* because they always want to be doing something.

This is where I had to make some major changes in my relationship plan, in order to reduce the amount of time I was allocating to this group. *Casual Friends* like to socialize with you and enjoy laughs together, but that does not mean they will be there for you in times of need—that was the revelation I discovered in my time of need. These friends were nowhere to be found. Some things that have worked for me to reallocate time with this group are:

- Limiting the number of gatherings with this group to a set frequency, i.e., every other month, once a quarter, a limited number of subscription or season tickets, etc.
- Not deviating from the frequency boundaries except for very special celebrations or events
- Not becoming the sole social planner for groups of casual friends

- Setting boundaries around too-frequent, impromptu visits

Initiating and Cultivating New Acquaintances

FIVE WAYS TO WELL-BEING

After Teresa's death, I became acutely aware of how important it is to be adding new people to our lives regularly. The importance of making new friends is reinforced in scientific research, which shows that on average, we lose half of our close network friends every seven years.[7] While this may sound unbelievable, think about how many of your classmates and/or wedding attendants you are or were still connected with after seven years.

We have already seen the evidence from the numerous scientific research reports that show how critical connection with people is for our overall well-being. Coupled with this turnover rate of friendships, it means that initiating and cultivating new relationships really should be a prioritized and an ongoing way of life for everyone.

Meeting new people can be exciting or intimidating, depending on your personality and your situation. While this is a very easy and normal act for most children, it becomes a less natural thing to do as we become adults. We may regularly meet new acquaintances through work and activities, but we are "too busy" or "introverted" or afraid to take the next step to see if these acquaintances can grow into more meaningful and nourishing friendships.

It is a numbers game—you are not going to like everyone, nor is everyone going to like you. Just keep in mind that ALL humans want to be happy and feel loved. So just go for it, and if it does not work out, you just let it go with nothing to lose. Just be sure to give it enough time before letting go, as it does take time and work to develop a friendship. The important thing to remember is that the objective is to develop meaningful relationships over the long run, and not just lots of acquaintances that often do not go any further after the initial meeting.

Some of the things I do that seem to be effective in meeting new people are:

- Getting involved in things that interest you. Whether it is classes, group activities, travels, or volunteer opportunities, you will be around people with something in common, making starting a conversation much easier.
- Tracking down old friends with whom you would like to reconnect. You can usually do this through social media or mutual friends, and then initiate a reconnection with them.
- Having confidence, because in reality, most people want to talk to people. We have just become overly paranoid of talking to strangers. Most of the time they will welcome you because you are taking the pressure off them to take the lead.
- Taking time to introduce yourself and thank a stranger or acquaintance who has helped you in some way.

- Getting in the habit of smiling and saying hello as you pass people you do not know. No one is invisible! Even if this person does not become a friend, it costs nothing and can make a huge difference in a person's day.
- Practicing your "starting conversations" with unknown customer service people. They are always open to talking with strangers and represent no risk to you.
- Facilitating conversational starters with remarks on the surroundings or occasion, or by giving a compliment, noting any obvious commonalities followed with a question, or by asking open-ended questions that begin with who, where, when, what, why, and how.

When you meet someone for the first time, that person starts in the outermost circle as an acquaintance. If you somehow "click" with each other, the next thing you need to do with a new acquaintance is to open up about something that is a little bit more personal than what you've already discussed. This way they show you if they are interested and receptive, simply by whether or not they disclose something about themselves in return.

Always have presence and a smile in your communication, listening closely with good eye contact if applicable, body language that shows interest, and brief, interjected, acknowledging comments. Focus on the conversation, not on what your next comment or response will be.

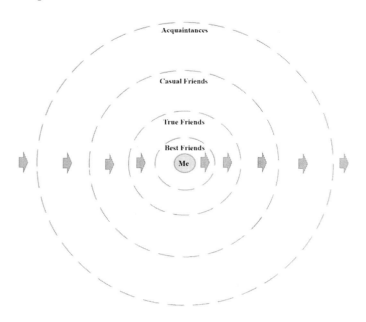

I find one of the easiest ways to start exchanging more with this person is by sharing a bit of news that may be of interest to them through a call, text, or e-mail. This serves as a good first step before inviting that acquaintance to go for coffee or lunch, a walk, shopping, a movie, etc.

Meeting new people takes time. Just as I do with nurturing my existing friendships, I put time on the calendar to go to places where I have opportunities to meet new acquaintances. Once I have met someone, I also notate reminders for myself to connect in some way to determine whether a cultivation is viable or not. If it is, then I initiate a "next connect time" so we can continue to get to know each other better. If it appears the acquaintance is not interested, I let it go for the sake of time and energy.

Do not get discouraged—remember, it is a numbers game. The more attempts you make, the more likely you are to have success. Remember, not all acquaintances move to inward rings; in fact, most do not.

Deemphasizing Negative-Energy Relationships

Our relationships are an essential component of our health, happiness, and overall well-being. As life evolves, things happen both in our lives and in others' that change us as part of the natural growing process. As a result of change, some relationships that worked well before may become disconnected or even toxic.

For troubled relationships, it is important to consider what each brings to your life before you decide if you want to put forth efforts to reconcile or deemphasize. If you decide you would feel more at ease, happier, and more content without this person in your life, consider deemphasizing the relationship. If you cannot decide, ask someone you trust for their opinion, as sometimes their perspective is helpful because they are not as close to the situation.

Any relationship that makes you feel dissatisfied, or worse about yourself instead of better, does not have to be accepted. It is up to each of us to find the courage to act on relationships that are no longer working. While this may sound selfish, it is not. It is important to be true to ourselves, and honest to these people, by being open about what it is that bothers us.

We are not in this world to be unhappy; we are here to have inner peace by being kind and loving to each other. If someone is so unhappy or angry that they cannot accept help or love, move on, but remain compassionate to those from whom you walked away. We never know what the future will bring. The two of you may ultimately reconnect at some point.

Actually, tension in friendships is not really that unusual. In fact, according to an extensive survey conducted in 2011 by Today.com and *SELF* magazine, "84 percent of women said that they have had at least one venomous friend who has brought toxicity into the relationship through belittling, backstabbing, or judging."[8]

The thing I get asked most often about is the best way to deemphasize relationships. Much of this depends on the situation, but also on your style. What works for one person may not feel comfortable at all to another. Pick the approach that you can do with confidence because, while difficult, it is even more draining to stay in a relationship that is no longer working for either of you.

There are two ways to end a relationship—either directly or passively. The most decent way is to be direct, open, and honest. It is important to clearly state your wish to end the relationship while being respectful of the other person and sensitive to the resulting emotions. If two people have had a satisfying and close relationship, they owe it to themselves and to each other to be forthright and fair about communicating during the final stage of the relationship. Direct approaches can be in person, in writing, or on the phone.

Some people do not feel comfortable with the direct approach. In that case, the passive option is basically to let the relationship taper off by not getting in touch or returning phone calls, instead of breaking things off officially. There is not a right or wrong to either approach, but before opting for one, do think about how you would prefer to be approached if the roles were reversed.

Once you've decided on your approach, the message you convey will vary with the situation. Common explanations may be:

- I am not happy in the relationship any longer because it does not seem to be working, so it would be better if we take a break or cut ties.
- A friendship has to be two-way, and ours has suffered from neglect.
- As people change, friendships change. What brought us together does not exist any longer.

However you end it, disconnect with love and compassion. This means not speaking negatively about the person. If you are asked about the person, you can honestly reply that you have not seen him/her, but you hope they are doing well.

My Action Plan and Associated Calendar

I am often asked for a sample of what a real action plan and calendar looks like. Here are some abbreviated samples from my own plan and calendar:

My Relationship Action Plan

RELATIONSHIP ACTION PLAN FOR THE YEAR

WHAT	WHO	HOW	WHEN
Cherish My Best Friends	Lew	1) Monthly Catch-up; 2) Important Reminders; 3) Birthday; 4) Commitment Discussion	1) N/A - everyday; 2) test on March 24th; 3) July 26th; 4) Around Jan 26th
	Maggie	1) Monthly Catch-up; 2) Important Reminders; 3) Birthday; 4) Commitment Discussion	1) 2nd each month; 2) daughter's wedding Oct 3rd; 3) April 2nd; 4) Around Oct 2nd
	Carla	1) Monthly Catch-up; 2) Important Reminders; 3) Birthday; 4) Commitment Discussion	1) 11th each month; 2) Surgery March 29th; 3) April 11th; 4) Around Nov 11th
	ETC.		
Recognize My Significant Other As #1	Lew	1) Above plus: 2) Venus and Mars reminders; 2) Five Love Languages quiz and discussion; 3) Anniversary day plan and discussion	1) Above plus: 2) Read insight card each Sunday night; 3) Quiz and discussion near anniversary - Sep 23rd; 4) Plan Sep 23rd together
Connect Regularly with True Friends	Viola	1) Quarterly Catch-up; 2) Important Reminders; 3) Birthday; 4) Commitment Discussion	1) 20th in June, Sep, Dec; 2) N/A as of now; 3) March 20th; 4) Around Sep 20th
	Nora	1) Quarterly Catch-up; 2) Important Reminders; 3) Birthday	1) 28th in April, July, Oct; 2) Italy Trip March 9th; 3) Jan 28th
	Jane	1) Quarterly Catch-up; 2) Important Reminders; 3) Birthday; 4) Commitment Discussion	1) 29th in June, Sep, Dec; 2) N/A as of now; 3) Sep 29th; 4) Around March 29th
	ETC.		
Manage Casual Friends Time	Quarterly Groups	Limit groups - this year only gourmet and theater	Gourmet - Feb, June, Aug, Nov; Theater - March, May, July, Oct
	Classes	Limit classes to those related to ACT 2	Blogging - Oct 23; Webinars - Feb 7th, June 3rd; Writers' Conference - Sep7-9th
	Outings w/ Others	Ladies' nights for dinner - try to make same time frames that Lew has obligations	Ladies' Group 1 - Feb 24th, May 18th, Aug 5th, Nov 1st; Ladies' Group 2 - Mar 3rd, Jun 14th, Sep 18th, Dec 3rd
Initiate and Cultivate New Acquaintances	Common Interest People	Regularly attend meditation, exercise class, and be more talkative at networking events	Weekly Sun or Mon meditation; Tues and Thurs flow class; Monthly Women's Professional and BFC Assn.
Deemphasize Negative Relationships	Tammy	Letter explaining things have not improved	Before March 31st

116

Once you have this action plan in place, you are ready to start carrying it out. You need to be the driver to make this happen successfully, and the easiest way to do that is to have reminders on your calendar. This eliminates the continuous thinking of . . .

- Who has birthdays this month?
- When is Caty's daughter getting married? What is the date of Sallie's shoulder surgery?
- Who was it that I was supposed to call this week? This month?
- Where can I go where there is a good likelihood I'll meet a new person who has the greatest potential to become a friend?
- How can I get to know Hilga better? When can we get together to allow us time to talk more?
- Which three people should I invite as my guests to the women's conference three weeks from today?

I found that the easiest way to do this was to first make myself a **Relationship Plan Calendar** for the year. Once I had everything on there, I integrated it into my everyday calendar system. In order to take friendships seriously, you really do need to manage your time around it, without things falling through the cracks. Here is a month out of my relationship calendar so you have an idea of how it looks.

My Relationship Calendar

CURRENT MONTH

S	M	T	W	T	F	S
		1	2 Catch-up with Maggie	3 Ladies' Group 2 Dinner	4	5
6 Venus / Mars Card	7	8 Bon Voyage to Nora	9 Nora Leaves for Italy	10	11 Catch-up with Carla	12
13 Venus / Mars Card	14	15 Ladies' Dinner & Theater	16	17	18	19
20 Viola's Birthday Venus / Mars Card	21	22	23 Study treat for Lew	24 Lew's Test – Good Luck	25	26 Commit Talk with Jane
27 Venus / Mars Card	28 Call Carla before surgery	29 Carla's Surgery	30	31		

14
Keeping Life Meaningful

My trifecta of losses was devastating. Having experienced both death and divorce in my life, it equaled that kind of emotional trauma, but threefold in a short period of time.

Harry S. Truman once said that "a pessimist is one who makes difficulties of his opportunities, and an optimist is one who makes opportunities of his difficulties." Now, years later, it is clear that I did in fact make opportunities of my difficulties.

There are two things that I do very differently in my life now:

1. I make time each day for quiet serenity and to set stress boundaries in my life by intentionally assessing and accepting what I can and cannot change. My quiet time can vary from meditation to early morning walks in nature, journaling, or even reading something inspirational and simply reflecting. On the days when I am feeling more stressed, I actually stop and put the Serenity Prayer into action using the three simple steps in the *Serenity Steps Approach* described earlier in the book:

1. I write down the problem that is keeping me from serenity.
2. I list the associated things that I can and cannot change.
3. I list the associated actions that I will take to get closer to serenity.

By following this simple lifestyle change, I not only still my mind each day so I intentionally keep my mind from jumping all over, but I also reduce the stress in my life by not worrying about things I cannot change and instead focus my time and efforts on things where I can make a difference.

> **Buddha was asked, 'What have you gained from meditation?'**
>
> **He replied, 'Nothing! However, let me tell you what I have lost:**
> **Anger, Anxiety, Depression, Insecurity, Fear of old age and death.'**
>
> 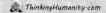 ThinkingHumanity·com

2. I consciously surround myself with relationships, both new and old, that ultimately yield greater happiness, better health, and overall well-being. Having learned whom I can really count on in my rings of relationships and therefore how important it is to consciously allocate my time with people accordingly, I lay out my relationship plan for the year and tweak it annually as necessary. Based on my lesson of misallocating my relationship time in the past, I design my plan for the year to achieve six complementary objectives:

1. Cherish my best friends
2. Recognize my significant other as number one in my life
3. Connect regularly with my true friends
4. Manage my time spent with casual friends
5. Initiate and cultivate new acquaintances
6. Deemphasize my negative-energy relationships

As demonstrated earlier in the book, I assign specific names (WHO) from my **Relationship Compass**, as well as WHAT, WHEN, and HOW for each of these objectives. While this sounds like a lot of work, it does not take much time, and has proven itself in guiding me to spend my time and energy where it matters.

Top Regrets When Dying

It is sad that so many people pass away with regrets. We owe it to ourselves to make the best of life in the present, rather than delaying things to the future with the thought that we can do things differently later. Who knows when that day will come?

Bronnie Ware, a former palliative nurse, wrote a book entitled *The Top Five Regrets of the Dying*. The book is based on common themes that surfaced when she talked to terminal patients about any regrets they had or anything they would do differently. Here are the most common top five:

1. I wish I'd had the courage to live a life true to myself, not the life others expected of me.
2. I wish I didn't work so hard.
3. I wish I'd had the courage to express my feelings.

4. I wish I had stayed in touch with my friends.
5. I wish that I had let myself be happier.

Note that expressing feelings and staying in touch with friends are both on the list. Many patients attributed being caught up in their own lives to why they let friendships slip away. There is a saying that if you spend quality time with the people you love, the relationships will grow stronger; but if you don't, they'll slowly fade away.

At this stage in life, nothing (money, status, material belongings, etc.) matters except making your feelings known to those you love. Unfortunately, because not everyone realizes the benefits of meaningful relationships until too late, often it is not possible to track down people quickly enough to express feelings before death.

Bronnie Ware, the author of the book, has a mantra we can all use to help us from having regrets not only at death, but in everyday life . . .

Life is a choice. It is YOUR life.
Choose consciously, choose wisely, choose
honestly. Choose happiness!

Make It Lasting

Sadly, lessons we learn are often short lived. Do you remember how, after so many lost loved ones in the 9/11 disaster, there seemed to be an increased awareness to reprioritize what and who is important, and to live each day to its fullest?

The events of 9/11 caused America to promise, "We will never forget." This meant to never forget the victims, to never forget the many heroic actions of helpers, and to never forget how that day felt.

For a while, in the wake of the tragedy, Americans did unite. They showed more appreciation for their freedoms and prosperity; numerous volunteers were helping to clean up Ground Zero; people began volunteering for both 9/11-related causes as well as others; people prioritized the loved ones in their lives; thousands of people returned to churches in an attempt to find peace with what had happened; and charitable donations increased as well.

But as time passed, both the horrific event and the lessons learned from it became a faded memory. Some of the changes lasted only a few months; church attendance went back to normal by November. Other changes, especially volunteerism, lasted a few years. While some scars of that day remain, most of our lives have largely returned to where they were before 9/11.

Each anniversary we call to mind the events of that day: the horror we felt as the towers crashed, the sadness of mourning loved ones, and the renewed appreciation for the freedoms we enjoy. Social media posts become viral each 9/11 with sentiment sharing such as . . .

At this moment x years ago, millions of Americans went to bed quietly, with no thought that the next morning their world would change forever. That night hundreds packed flight bags they would not live to open. Thousands slept with loved ones for the last time. One never knows what a new day has in store. Let us live each day to the fullest, and never miss a chance to let those dearest to us know of our love for them. So tonight if you have someone in your life that you love, tell them.

But just remembering annually is not enough. Unfortunately, senseless tragedies are a part of life. Similar feelings and the question of why also occurred after the fall of Nazi Germany in the 1940s, the Columbine High massacre in 1999, and the 2012 shootings at Sandy Hook Elementary. The same is true of natural tragedies, like the unexpected loss of my friend Teresa.

The key is to put what you learn into action. The lesson learned may be different for each of us. Whether it is to make daily quiet time for serenity, more openly express your feelings to those important to you, spend more time with friends and family, or something else, the important thing is to not miss the opportunity to learn and grow from the tragedy.

Nancy M. Forbes

Finding Time

Perhaps the most common excuse for not developing new habits evolves around not having time, or being too busy. It actually is quite comical how "busy" people perceive themselves as being.

We all have the same twenty-four hours each day, seven days a week, and three hundred sixty-five days per year. It all comes down to what you want to do, and thus how you prioritize your time. H. Jackson Brown, Jr.—the author best known for his inspirational book, *Life's Little Instruction Book*—captured the complete absurdity of not having enough time in his quote that compares the amount of time that some of the world's greatest innovators had.

> Don't say you don't have enough time. You have exactly the same number of hours per day that were given to Helen Keller, Pasteur, Michelangelo, Mother Teresa, Leonardo Da Vinci, Thomas Jefferson, and Albert Einstein.
>
> - H. Jackson Brown, Jr.

It is a fact that nobody has time to do everything, but we do have time to do what's most important to us. We all make choices about how we spend our time. Each of us decides what we value the most, and then we make trade-offs between what we make time to do versus what we choose not to do. Making time for the important thing is a result of prioritizing.

It comes down to two options: (1) Prioritize and make time; or (2) do not prioritize and regret once it is too late.

Don't Wait Until It Is Too Late

So one more time . . . close your eyes. Take a deep breath or two to relax. Reflect on a recent time you had with one of your closer friends . . . it can be a fun time, a sad time, a relaxation time, a reflective time, etc. Picture where you were, who you were with, what you were doing, what you were wearing, and so on. Enjoy reminiscing for a bit and then open your eyes.

Think about how you would feel if that person were no longer here tomorrow. Would you be longing for one more conversation to tell them some things you wish you had already expressed? Would you wish you had spent less time dwelling on things you could not change and more time with this person? Does this exercise make you want to rethink with whom and on what you spend your time?

It is my hope that after reading this book, not only will you have a better appreciation of how you can better prioritize the important things in life through serenity-based stress reduction, but also have more insight into the people in your life, and how you can have more time to find, keep, and surround yourself with relationships that yield better health, greater happiness, and overall well-being.

Acknowledgments

Prior to my trifecta of challenges, I could never understand how people could welcome difficult situations, regarding them as growth opportunities for which to be grateful. But through my journey, I learned to still my mind, to recognize and accept my scope of control, and to trust God. Yes, I still have to work on these things regularly, but I now accept that I am not in control of the bigger plan in life. As Norman Vincent Peale once said, "Whenever God wants to send you a gift, He wraps it up in a problem." So first and foremost, I thank God for my "gifts."

Secondly, I would not even have a story to tell if not for my trifecta of losses; it was through this heart wrenching time that I learned many kinds of boundaries, including those that divide the people and things that matter most, and how important it is to prioritize my time and efforts there with intention. Thank you Tracy, Lew, friends and family, and former work colleagues, for teaching me where to draw the lines.

I am not sure if I could have written the book without the support and encouragement of some wonderful people in my life. Thank you Dr. F, Dr. R, and Dr. P for your professional help and coaching. Thank you Lew, Zack, and Tyler for your patience, presence and encouragement throughout all of the losses. Thank you Elaine, Marcy, Deborah, Kathy E., Suzanne, Margaret, Deanna, Astrid, Trish, my YaYas, and Yoko for regularly checking on me during those difficult months, and reminding me that tough times do not last, but tough people do.

Having never taken on something like writing a book, I knew that I needed to surround myself with a group of people with whom I could collaborate on concepts, titles, topics; pre-read early versions; test ideas; and tap for professional expertise when needed. In alphabetical order with hopes of not forgetting anyone, thank you Amiet, Anita, Cathy, Christine, Dawn, Edith, Elaine, Hilary, Jan, Jana, JoEllen, Laura, Lauren G., Lauren J., Lew, Lois, Mary, Paul, Rebecka, Roni, Sandra, Sarah, Tina, Trish, Tyler, and Zack.

The book would not be what it is without the great thinking of minds like those of John F. Kennedy, Tyler Perry, Mary Stevenson, Joseph Campbell, John Kabat-Zinn, Shasta Nelson, Reinhold Niebuhr, F. W. Boreham, H. Jackson Brown Jr., Zig Ziglar, World Fellowship of Buddhists, Trent Shelton, Jacqueline Olds, MD, Richard S. Schwartz, MD, the producers of the General Social Survey, John Gray, Gary D. Chapman, and Bronnie Ware.

I start each morning with prayer, gratitude, inspiration and meditation. I find constant inspiration from the newsletters and daily devotions I look forward to each day from my three "inspiration regulars." Thank you Mike Dooley for *Notes from the Universe* (http://www.tut.com/Inspiration/nftu), Greg Kennard for *SpiritJava* (http://nspireoutreach.org/media), and Sarah Young for *Jesus Calling, Devotions for Every Day of the Year.*

And last but certainly not least, I thank all of you who have been there through the story and/or through the book in a subtler way, you have made a huge difference (you know who you are) . . . I could not have done it without you. Thank you!

TOOLS AND RESOURCES

Further Readings

- *Big Picture Partnering*, Dr. Jan Hoistad (2004)

- **Buddhism and Meditation for the Modern World**, http://kadampa.org/

- **"Footprints in the Sand,"** Mary Stevenson (1939), http://www.footprints-inthe-sand.com/

- *Friendships Don't Just Happen!*, Shasta Nelson (2013)

- **Getting Started with Meditation**, http://aboutmeditation.com/getting-started-with-meditation/

- **How to Meditate**, http://www.how-to-meditate.org/

- *Jesus Calling: Enjoying Peace in His Presence*, Sarah Young (2004)

- *Life's Little Instruction Book*, H. Jackson Brown, Jr. (1991)

- *Mary & Me*, Mary Potter Kenyon and Mary Jedlicka Humston (2015)

- **Meditation 101**, http://life.gaiam.com/article/meditation-101-techniques-benefits-beginner-s-how

- *Men Are from Mars, Women Are from Venus*, John Gray (1992)

- *Mindfulness for Beginners: Reclaiming the Present Moment—and Your Life*, Jon Kabat-Zinn (2012)

- **Notes from the Universe**, Mike Dooley, Daily Brief Inspirational Emails, http://www.tut.com/Inspiration/nftu

- **Serenity Prayer**, Karl Paul Reinhold Niebuhr, https://en.wikipedia.org/wiki/Serenity_Prayer

- **SpiritJava**, Gregg Kennard, Daily Inspirational Messages, http://nspireoutreach.org/media

- *The Five Love Languages*, Gary D. Chapman (2004)

- *The Friendship Crisis*, Marla Paul (2004)

- *The Happiness Project*, Gretchen Rubin (2011)

- *The Happiness Trap*, Russ Harris (2007)

- *The Lonely American*, Jacqueline Olds, MD, and Richard S. Schwartz, MD (2009)

- *The Top Five Regrets of the Dying*, Bronnie Ware (2012)

- *Vital Friends*, Tom Rath (2006)

- *Wherever You Go, There You Are*, Jon Kabat-Zinn (1994)

Serenity Steps
Approach Action Plan

Create your own plan of action for whatever problem(s) you are facing. Put the Serenity Prayer into action with three simple steps:

1. List the **PROBLEM** keeping you from serenity. <u>Use a separate sheet for additional problems</u>.
2. List the associated things that you **CAN CHANGE** and those you **CANNOT CHANGE**. Blank rows allow for additional **CAN**s and **CANNOT**s if needed.
3. List the associated **ACTIONS** you will take for each change to bring you closer to serenity, adding as many bullets as needed.

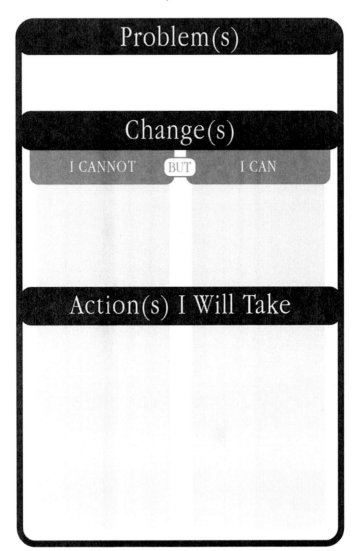

Problem(s)

Change(s)

I CANNOT   BUT   I CAN

Action(s) I Will Take

Serenity Steps
Approach Helpful Hints

If you are having problems filling out your action plan worksheet, assist your thinking by asking questions. This helps us be able to look more deeply at issues, break them into parts, find blind spots, etc.

Questions to Help Boost Your Critical Thinking:

1. What is the problem?
2. What is the goal?
3. What information is essential?
4. What do I know for sure?
5. What do I not know?
6. Is this fact or opinion?
7. Who else does this problem/situation affect?
8. Who else should be involved in this decision?
9. Can I view this from another perspective?
10. Have I played devil's advocate?
11. What are the alternatives?

12. What have I taken for granted?
13. Am I trying to reach a conclusion too quickly?
14. What is the big picture?
15. How are my emotions affecting my thoughts?
16. Does the problem make sense?
17. Am I putting my own interests in front of others'?
18. What is the worst-case scenario?
19. Have I let my gut feeling direct my thoughts?
20. What are the risks?
21. What are the future implications?
22. Do I have control over the outcome?
23. Does anyone have a hidden agenda?
24. Are the sources credible?
25. If I proceed with my idea, what might be the conclusion?
26. If I do not proceed with my idea, what might be the conclusion?
27. Am I focusing on trivial issues rather than the big picture?
28. Is the argument fair?
29. Is the argument relevant?
30. Is the argument credible?
31. Do the advantages outweigh the risks?

32. Who is responsible for what and when?
33. What will success look like?
34. Have I clearly articulated my position?
35. When did the problem start?
36. What has changed about the situation?
37. Is improvement possible?
38. What is missing?
39. Do I need additional information?

Relationship Assessment Survey

Respond to the four statements below for each relationship in your life *today*, not in the past or desired future.

1. **The phrase that best describes <u>how you usually communicate</u> with this person is:**
    Choose one of the following answers:

    a) Without any regularity
    b) Occasionally via the phone, in person, or social media
    c) Regularly, when brought together by some common activity requiring interaction
    d) Regularly, when brought together by some common activity, but conversations are expanded to include social communication as well
    e) Regularly, driven not by a defined activity but by a desire by both of you to be in touch, whether in person or otherwise

2. **The phrase that best describes <u>the deepest level of communication</u> you have with this person is:**
   Choose one of the following answers:

   a) Few words other than perhaps polite greetings
   b) General small talk
   c) Sharing personal information with each other
   d) Sharing opinions and beliefs with each other
   e) Sharing values, feelings, and confessions that require courage and vulnerability to bring up

3. **The phrase that best describes <u>the highest level of support you provide to each other</u>:**
   Choose one of the following answers:

   a) No effort to support; content with exchange of basic and general knowledge about each other
   b) One-way effort to support and encourage, not reciprocated by the other
   c) Two-way effort to praise *and encourage each other* on achievements and accomplishments

   d) Two-way effort to support and coach each other to reach life goals

   e) Two-way effort to prioritize openly and honestly to help each other achieve a deeper understanding of self

4. The phrase that best describes <u>the highest level of energy you experience after interacting</u> with this person is:

Choose one of the following answers:

   a) No feeling of energy because of minimal interaction

   b) A feeling of relief that you recognize someone's face or voice on the phone in a group of strangers

   c) An interest to keep getting to know each other more and more

   d) The excitement and enjoyment of sharing deeper communications and new experiences together

   e) The heartfelt, reflective, and energized feeling after being open and vulnerable with someone you trust

<u>See www.nancymforbes.com for survey details.</u>

Relationship
Commitment Discussion Guide

Discuss with interested BEST and some TRUE friends once per year about six months after their birthday.

Hi _____. (Get comfortable with about ten to fifteen minutes of chitchat to catch up.) Then go into commitment discussion below . . .

A meaningful friendship is very much a two-way effort. I believe it is important to be in sync with friendship expectations, what is working, and what we can do differently with our relationship IN THE YEAR AHEAD. I invited you to have this discussion so we can do just that. All I have are four questions for us to discuss, and hopefully it will be interesting and informative for both of us.

1. What do you think about the way we usually communicate, i.e., frequency, regularity, desire, etc.? Is there anything you would like to change about it?

_____

_____

_____

_____

_____

_____

2. How do you feel about the depth of our communication, i.e., small talk, personal sharing, opinions and beliefs, and sharing values/feelings/confessions that require courage and vulnerability to bring up? Are you comfortable with where it is, or would you like something different?

_____

_____

_____

_____

_____

_____

3. There is a wide spectrum of support friends can provide to each other, ranging from one- or two-way support and encouragement, coaching each other, and even helping each other achieve a deeper understanding of self. Where do you think we are, and is that where you want us to stay this next year?

    _____

    _____

    _____

    _____

    _____

    _____

4. How do you usually feel after we interact, either by phone or in person, i.e., nothing, interest to get to know each other better, enjoyment of sharing deeper communications and new experiences, or heartfelt, reflective, and energized after being open and vulnerable with someone you trust? Are you satisfied, or do you want to try to strive for more in this area?

    _____

    _____

    _____

Book Discussion Guide

1. If you take the time to still your body and mind, you will find you **receive** instructions instead of **asking** for directions. In what capacity do you exercise being still each day? If you do not take time to be still, what is preventing you?

2. Nancy talks of how she put the Serenity Prayer into action by finding boundaries through what she could and could not change. In what areas do you find yourself wasting time and energy on things outside of your control?

3. Our fast-paced life has made many people looking for "quick fixes" rather than having to put time and effort into resolving conflict. Recall some instances where your perseverance paid off.

4. Nancy expressed sadness and surprise that she had not realized that Teresa was a best friend until it was too late. How much time have you spent intentionally reflecting on your relationships? How frequently do you do this?

5. It is important to balance your time and effort with people based on the meaningfulness of the relationship. Do you think you would find the kind of imbalance Nancy discovered if you differentiated your relationships between Best Friends, True Friends, Casual Friends, and Acquaintances? Where would those imbalances be?

6. Do you take the time and effort to make your feelings known to those people closest to you—before it is too late? In what ways?

7. Nancy presented many facts to point out that the influence of social relationships on risk for mortality is comparable with well-established risk factors such as smoking, alcohol, obesity, etc. Why do you think that this is not more well known? If it were, how do you think this would change the amount of time people make for meaningful relationships?

8. We often identify ourselves in association with the work we do in or outside of the home. Describe how you would feel about your identity if suddenly you were told that your skills were no longer needed.

9. Recall when you were first attracted to your significant other and how giving you likely were. Imagine a tipping scale. Would you say that the scale is now even or tilted in how giving you are to your significant other? If you are giving less, are you at the risk of taking him/her for granted?

10. The book is filled with quotations. Is there a quotation that resonated with you, and if so, why?

Notes

1. Tyler Perry's Facebook page, accessed September 6, 2016, https://www.facebook.com/TylerPerry/.

2. Holt-Lunstad J, Smith TB, Layton JB. Social Relationships and Mortality Risk: A Meta-Analytic Review. *PLoS Medicine*, 2010; 7 (7): e1000316 DOI: 10.1371/journal.pmed.1000316

3. Holwerda, T. J. Deeg, D., Beekman, A. van Tilburg, T. G., Stek, M. L., Jonker, C., and Schoevers, R. 2012. Research paper: Feelings of loneliness, but not social isolation, predict dementia onset: results from the Amsterdam Study of the Elderly (AMSTEL) *Journal of Neurology, Neurosurgery and Psychiatry*.

4. Luo, Y, Hawkley, L. C., Waite, L. J., Cacioppo, J. T. Loneliness, Health, and Mortality in Old Age: A National Longitudinal Study. *Social Science & Medicine*, 2012; Volume 74, Issue 6, March 2012, Pages 907–914.

5. Lechman, J. F., Carter, C. S., Hennessy, M. B., Hrdy, S. B., Keverne, E. B., Klann-Delius, G., Schradin, C., Todt, D., von Holst, D. Group Report: Biobehavioral Processes in Attachment and Bonding. *Attachment and Bonding: A New Synthesis*, 2005 (MIT PRESS) Carter, C. S., Ahnert, L., Grossmann, K. E., Hrdy, S. B., Lamb, M. E., Porges, S.W., Sachser, N.; 337.

6. McPherson, M., Smith-Lovin, L., and Brashears, M. E. Social Isolation in America: Changes in Core Discussion Networks over Two Decades. *American Sociological Review*, 2006; 71; 353 DOI: 10.1177/000312240607100301.

7. Mollenhorst, G., Volker, B., Flap, V. Social Contexts and Personal Relationships: The Effect of Meeting Opportunities on Similarity for Relationships of Different Strength. NWO (Netherlands Organization for Scientific Research). *ScienceDaily*, 2009; www.sciencedaily.com/releases/2009/05/0905271 11907.htm.

8. TODAY.com and SELF.com. Toxic Friends Survey. Toxic Relationships, *Psychology Today*, 2011.

About the Author

Nancy M. Forbes is an author, a sought-after speaker, and personal lifestyle coach who delights in helping others deliberately take time to evaluate where and with whom they are spending their valuable time and energy. After a successful career in the corporate world, Nancy had to delay launching the "ACT 2" she had envisioned in order to navigate a trifecta of personal losses. She shares her experience and simple and effective techniques for finding serenity, transforming

seemingly adverse conditions into opportunities for personal growth and regret mitigation in her book *The Serenity Mindset: A Personal Guide for Prioritizing People and Things That Matter*. When not practicing what she teaches, Nancy lives in Marietta, Georgia, and enjoys spending time with her husband and grown sons, as well as travelling, playing in the dirt, arts and entertainment, hiking, and spending time with family and friends.